LEADERSHIP FOR THE NEW FEMALE MANAGER

21 POWERFUL STRATEGIES FOR COACHING HIGH-PERFORMANCE TEAMS, EARNING RESPECT & INFLUENCING UP

KARINA G. SANCHEZ

Virago

PUBLISHING

www.CorporateToFreelancer.com

Published by Virago Publishing

Virago
PUBLISHING

DEDICATION

To my two leaders, Valentina, and Andre, who are my daily dose of inspiration and a reminder of the kind of leader I aspire to be.

"You're never too young to change the world."

SPECIAL BONUS!

Want this cheatsheet for FREE?

You'll learn how to:
- Believe you can!
- Learn the rules & how to play them
- What to do in meetings
- How to be authentic to yourself
- Crush your fear

FREE

5 PRINCIPLES OF PERSONAL BRANDING

THE ESSENTIAL CHECKLIST FOR NEW FEMALE MANAGERS!

LEADERSHIP EXPERT

The Empowered Leader

Get FREE unlimited access to it and all of my books by joining our community!

Scan with your camera to join!

In the *5 Golden Rules to Personal Branding,* you'll find:

- The easy-to-follow golden rules will help you design your brand from scratch.

- My personal story took 20 years to develop through many mistakes, time, and sacrifice.
- Quick action steps that you can take right now to get started.
- A quick access to our community of amazing female leaders to help you form your tribe.

INTRODUCTION

"We don't need a title to lead. We need to care. People would rather follow a leader with a heart than a leader with a title."
    ~ Craig Groeschel

As Groeschel suggests in his quote, titles don't make leaders. We would rather follow those that truly care about people.

To a certain extent, a title does come with some authority. That doesn't mean others will instantly follow you; it certainly doesn't make you a good leader. You have to take personal responsibility for this, and it means dedicating time to learning the craft of leadership. It's a journey that's worth committing to.

Titles give clues about our status in the world, but

they don't truly provide key information about our person or expertise. An unmarried woman is often addressed as

'Miss,' but a married woman as 'Mrs.' *What do those titles really tell us about a woman?*

In short, they tell us nothing...

There's a possibility that someone with the title Mrs. is no longer married but chose to keep the title and surname.

Titles certainly don't tell us if you're a good mother, a hard worker, or a great leader. The title of Mrs. alone simply indicates a person is—or was once—married. Even the title of Doctor simply indicates medical or educational attainment, but it alone tells us nothing about a person's nature or expertise.

That's why Groeschel's quote is so on point—anyone can be labeled a leader, but a title alone doesn't indicate anything. Only YOU get to decide what type of leader you will be!

To be a great leader, you have to want it. You have to care. People will respect and follow you if you have heart and passion—and if you truly care. While many leaders want to become great, it's easy to lose sight of how we can develop into the great leader we want to become. This is often because being a leader brings responsibilities and stresses you've never faced before, especially if you're an early-career leader.

So, ask yourself now, *do you have the heart to become a great leader? Do you care enough?*

There are so many benefits of being a great leader.

Some of the world's most prestigious and highest-performing teams report that they perform well because of inspirational and caring leaders. We'll be exploring this in more detail throughout this book. Being a young leader can bring so much more to the table, but young leaders also face many unique challenges. They are often challenges new managers are unprepared for, through no fault of their own.

Many people want nothing more than to become great leaders... they just don't know which path they need to take. While they have many technical skills, some common problems young leaders encounter include not having much work experience and/or people skills. This can make many 'real' situations in the workplace overwhelming, and this is exactly the reason why being a leader that cares is important.

While creating this book, I spoke to some inspirational young leaders about their challenges when they first began their leadership journey. These key challenges arose from:

- Managing change in the workplace Lacking people skills and work experience
- Insufficient communication skills when it comes to communicating projects, delivering messages, and providing feedback to staff members
- An inability to effectively identify developmental areas for themselves and their team

- Resolving conflict and tension management
  Identifying growth and promotional opportunities for themselves and others within their team
- Developing presentation skills and improving as a result of their experience
- Getting to know their team and being able to read their body language and facial cues to avoid misunderstandings
- Developing their emotional intelligence to deal with difficult situations in a professional manner
- Improving time management and organization skills
- Being able to problem-prioritize effectively by using their evaluation skills based on business needs and goals
- Understanding the strengths and development areas within the team to assign work accordingly
- Building trust and being approachable to team members
- Focusing on the team and being aware of what is happening in the background
- Developing self-awareness of their own leadership

If you want to become a great leader, work must be done. While the above list of key issues may seem overwhelming, these are all common challenges that many early leaders face. On a positive note, these are all areas that you can work on and fix easily by applying the strategies in this book. You already have the technical skills, but this book will help you shine as a person and settle into the unique and inspirational leadership role you aspire to occupy or have been promoted to. That's why this

book focuses on helping you become the leader YOU want to be... not the leader you think other people want you to be. Make no mistake; there's a lot to learn if you want to become an inspirational leader. But it's worth gaining such a rewarding role.

If you're ready to develop killer leadership skills, master your coaching habits, and build trust while developing high-performance teams, read on. I got you! For too long, I have watched as early leaders faced their challenges alone. I can help you become committed to your leadership role, embrace the opportunities in front of you, and rise to meet all changes that cross your path. You are not alone, and I'm here to help you step into your greatness!

This book is split into four key sections to help you grow into your leadership role and become great at it. You'll first focus on developing and leading yourself. Then in section II, you'll consider how you can use your skills, instincts, and abilities to inspire and lead others. In section III, you'll dive deep into team leading and how you can use your skills to motivate your team, share your vision, and drive your team toward success. Finally, section IV provides you with extra tools so that you can continue to grow and develop. Remember, a great leader recognizes there's always something to learn and develop!

By the end of this book, you'll have all the tools you need to excel!

Above all else, you will learn to be your best!

You're probably wondering who I am and what qualifies me to write this book. Well, let me introduce myself. My name is Karina. I have worked with young leaders like yourself for the last twenty years. I've devoted my life to helping others succeed. It's not enough for me to work with organizations. I want to work with individual leaders, particularly early-career leaders who have all the technical skills they need but do not yet have the "people experience" that is so crucial to their success. I have seen many bright minds struggle in their roles because of this. Trying to navigate the unknowns of leadership—such as finding better ways of communicating with diverse teams, influencing up and across, and building trust. This is so much harder without knowing exactly how and where to start! I've spent my coaching and training career helping leaders find true success and fulfillment.

I've been fortunate enough to have lived in seven different countries where I owned and operated training, coaching, and mentorship businesses. I'm a keynote speaker and corporate trainer, and I deliver leadership training sessions in four languages. I've consulted in the tech, pharmaceutical, retail, and financial industries (just to name a few). Over the last 15 years, I have facilitated hundreds of in-person and virtual workshops worldwide.

I'm renowned for my energy and passion, and I bring about change by inspiring and motivating small and large teams. I have an uncanny way of opening minds to new possibilities, encouraging innovative ways of thinking, and helping individuals and companies manage their best

resource—the human resource. My work is not yet done as I continue to coach and mentor hundreds of new managers to excel in leadership roles and become successful within their organizations. I will undoubtedly impact the way you lead. My deepest passion is helping you become a goal-driven, forward-thinking, action-oriented leader. With me by your side, failure is not an option!

I aim to impact and inspire more leaders than ever by sharing my knowledge, experience, and expertise to help establish the next generation of incredibly inspiring and successful leaders.

But this book is not about me; it's about you. It's about you becoming the leader you aspire to be. It's time to take your motivation, instincts, and determination and use them to build your empire. Great leaders attract a great workforce and top-performing team members. The power to be a great leader lies within you! In the words of Brian Tracy:

"Become the kind of leader that people would follow voluntarily, even if you had no title or position."
~ Brian Tracy

Now it's time to head over to chapter 1. We'll begin your journey into excellent leadership by discussing how to lead yourself first. This is important because you must be able to lead yourself before leading others. It is, therefore, the first step if you want to excel as a leader. This book will change the way you view leadership and have you questioning and challenging your own style

and skills. It will give you the strength, confidence, and power you need to succeed in your role and beyond!

To embrace the next step of your journey, simply turn the page. Your destiny now lies in your own hands. *Are you ready?*

SECTION I – LEADING YOURSELF

As I mentioned, a great leader needs to be able to lead themselves. They also need to be able to recognize how they can improve and develop. A great leader teaches others how to develop. They are visionaries who prepare others for the future, and often help others map out their journey. But in order to do that, they first need to map out their own journey.

This section aims to do two things. To prepare you to become a great leader, and to inspire you to successfully lead others. It will encourage you to dig deep and find out what you really want. It will help you figure out how you can be the best version of yourself, clarify what you must overcome to get there, and encourage you to grow and develop your managerial skills.

This is the first step towards inspiring others to be the best versions of themselves. It's time to become a great leader who raises the next generation of great leaders!

THE MANAGER'S SWOT ANALYSIS

A Great Leader Knows How To Inspire And Motivate their team. If you want to lead a team effectively, you need to understand yourself deeper and consider the type of manager you are (or aspire to be). This means that you need to dig deep and establish your own:

- Strengths
- Gaps
- Blind spots
- Core passions
- Competencies

Once you identify these qualities in yourself, it becomes easier to recognize them in others. Being able to do this means you can help others grow and reach their full potential, which is what being a great leader is all about.

It's not always easy to assess ourselves, but once we learn this skill, we repeatedly return to it.

The question is, *how can you discover these qualities about yourself?*

WHY A SWOT ANALYSIS?

Understanding yourself better is a must; the most effective way to work this out is to use SWOT analysis. You may have heard of this already, but just in case you haven't, SWOT analysis is an easy-to-use framework that allows you to gauge your current performance and map out your future ambitions and potential. It prompts you to analyze four key areas:

- **S**trengths
- **W**eakness
- **O**pportunities
- **T**hreats

Let's clarify these areas further...

Strengths, these are the things you are good at already. They're your best attributes. By **weaknesses,** we mean you get to review areas in which you need to improve or develop. Sometimes in life, we face **opportunities,** but we may not make the most of them. That's why reviewing what they are and what are possible prompts us to be prepared to embrace any opportunities that present themselves to us. **Threats** are barriers that could delay us or even stop us from pursuing our path.

A SWOT analysis is a popular tool because it can be applied to most things. For example, you can apply it to:

1. Individuals
2. Teams
3. Projects
4. Organizations
5. Charities
6. Products

It also allows you to analyze your managerial abilities and determine whether you need to take action to tackle threats and embrace imminent opportunities. All you need to do is answer the questions while focusing on specific areas. Sometimes you may need to adjust the questions slightly— so that you can apply them to specific domains—but the underlying concept remains the same.

WHAT ARE THE ELEMENTS OF A SWOT ANALYSIS FOR YOUR LEADERSHIP STRENGTHS AND ABILITIES?

A SWOT analysis is your opportunity to take a confidential but rigorously honest look at your leadership skills and abilities. This allows you to plan your journey and be accountable for the quality of work you produce, increase your motivation, and strive towards your future goals. All of this is done while addressing any issues along the way. Remember that it's important to consider what you already do well because you deserve to be praised for your achievements so far!

It's not always easy to evaluate yourself. Many people find the process of highlighting what they're good at to be difficult. Others find it difficult to consider the things they are not good at. You can ask yourself several questions if you want to analyze your leadership abilities. Let's look at the elements of SWOT again, but this time we'll consider them from a leadership and management perspective.

Strengths

As mentioned earlier, your strengths focus on what you do well. There are a series of questions you can ask yourself to ensure you are aware of the things you do best. Ask yourself:

- Regarding leadership and management, what skills do I feel come naturally to me?
- Which tasks as a manager have I learned fastest, and which have been the easiest for me to pick up?
- If you asked others, which of my interpersonal skills would they value the most?

- What values and morals are important to me, and how do they help me perform better as a manager?

Weaknesses

Although it's sometimes difficult to consider the things we aren't good at, learning to assess the areas in which we need to develop and improve is an important skill. If we want to move forward, there's always something we can do better or learn that will help us. Things change in business constantly, so acknowledging the things we don't know can give us something to work towards. Ask yourself:

- What prevents me from delegating to others effectively?
- Am I happy with my approach if I don't perform as well as I think I should? How do I handle underperformance?
- What interpersonal challenges do I fear, and why?
- Are there any types of situations or people that I struggle to manage?

Opportunities

These things can allow you to grow your skills as a leader and can often be measured in your performance and your team's performance. Ask yourself:

- Are there any training opportunities available to me to help me overcome my weaknesses and any other barriers I am facing?
- Do I have access to any other management tools or frameworks, such as coaching? If so, am I able/willing to take advantage of them?
- Consider my direct reports. Are there any new ways I can develop their skills through delegation?
- What projects are on the horizon, and how can I develop my managerial skills in relation to them?

Threats

The threats you face can pose a risk to your success, growth, and performance. Threats are often simply presented as barriers. As a manager, you can use your problem-solving skills to overcome them. Ask yourself:

- What challenges do I face as a manager within the scope of an upcoming project? Do I need to develop any of my weaker areas before the project begins?
- Am I able to effectively influence my team and colleagues? What can I do to develop relationships with my current stakeholders if not?

- Are there any changes or challenges coming up soon that will test my leadership skills and ability to inspire?
- How can I manage my direct report's performance in a more effective and efficient way?

Your Practice Opportunity

Are you ready to take advantage of the opportunities presented to you?

It's now your time to access your talents, skills, strengths, and weaknesses by using the SWOT analysis template below. Use the questions to help you, and ensure you fill in at least one item per quadrant.

Being honest about your skills and weaknesses can help you build trust as a leader. This, in turn, can help you increase your self-confidence. You can use the SWOT analysis framework to assess your skills and those of your direct reports to help them develop and grow.

Remember...

"*The greatest leader is not necessarily the one who does the greatest things. He is the one that gets the people to do the greatest things.*"
~ Ronald Reagan

SWOT ANALYSIS

List your strengths, weaknesses, opportunities, and threats.

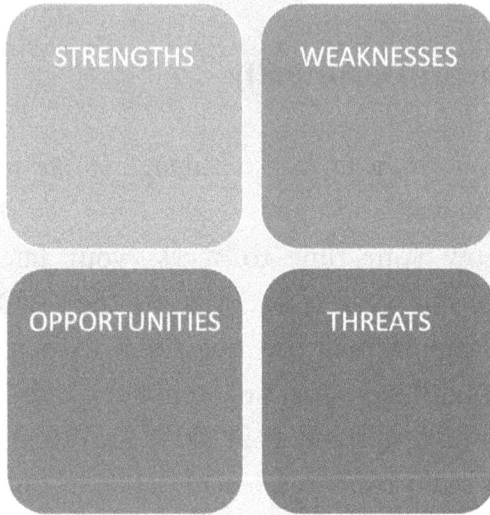

STRENGTHS	WEAKNESSES
OPPORTUNITIES	THREATS

QUESTIONS TO ASK

Strengths

- In what aspects of management and leadership do you feel like a 'natural?'

- What managerial tasks have you found easiest to pick up and learn quickly?
- What are your morals and values, and how do these make you a better manager?
- What do other people value you for in terms of interpersonal skills?

Weaknesses

- What interpersonal challenges are you most scared of dealing with?
- What stops you from delegating effectively?
- Are there particular types of people you struggle to manage?
- How do you handle underperformance? Are you happy with your approach?

Threats

- Are any projects coming up that may reveal weaknesses in your management ability?
- Do you need to manage a direct report's performance better to protect the organization?
- Is there an organizational change coming up that will test your ability to inspire?
- Can you effectively influence internally? If not, do you need to develop your relationships with key stakeholders?

Opportunities

- Are there management tools or frameworks you can take advantage of, such as coaching?
- Are there training opportunities that will allow you to address your weaknesses?
- What projects are coming up that will allow you to develop your managerial skills?
- Are there any new ways you can develop your direct reports through delegation?

GAINING SELF-CONFIDENCE AND SELF-TRUST

*E*very great leader needs to have a presence!

By presence, I mean they have a whole host of skills. But most of all, they enter the room and make an instant impact. People breathe a sigh of relief. They know this leader ensures things get done or is at least capable of delivering a plan of how to get there. They are the motivators, the problem solvers, and the instructors. They're cool under pressure and always appear to know what they are doing. *But what really gives those leaders presence?*

That's easy... they trust and have confidence in themselves.

In chapter one, we talked about assessing your strengths. So, you already have some confidence because you recognize that these are your assets. They're the things you do well. You are a leader because you deserve to be a leader. As you grow, you can grow your strengths and experience further.

Throughout this chapter, we'll explore building your self-confidence and trust in yourself. These are really important skills for a leader to master. Just like any important skill, building these takes time. So, this chapter will get you started, but it's up to you to continue this work as you develop in your leadership role.

It's time for you to take the reins and keep heading in the right direction!

WITHOUT CONFIDENCE, THERE'S NO LEADERSHIP

Let me ask you a serious question.

If you don't believe in yourself, who will?

Say your car breaks down, and two mechanics come to look at it. The first tells you they 'think' they can fix your car. They mumble something quietly to you, stand with their hands in their pockets, fidget, and avoid eye contact as they tell you what they 'think' the problem is, but then admit they aren't completely sure.

The second shows up with a smile, maintains eye contact, and stands up straight as he explains exactly what's wrong with your car. He even shows you the problem under the hood, confidently tells you he 'can' fix it quickly, and lets you know how much it will cost in parts and labor.

Whom do you choose? Of course, you're going to choose the second mechanic. But what's the difference?

Mechanic number 1 is sabotaging himself. He looks at the floor, fidgets, and mumbles. These aren't the actions of someone who believes in themselves and their own abilities. It's hard to trust someone who doesn't trust themselves.

The second mechanic is confidence. He stands up straight, he looks you in the eye, explains the problem, and even shows you where it is. There's no need to doubt him. He believes he can fix it because he trusts in his skills and abilities. As a result, you believe him too. He's the expert, after all. That's how your direct reports need to feel about you!

Like those mechanics, leaders who lack self-confidence will self-sabotage their leadership potential. You must lead others by first believing in yourself. By developing self-confidence and self-trust, great leaders:

- Become fearless
- Communicate confidently
- Have a constant flow of ideas
- Enhance work satisfaction
- Instil and improve follower trust
- Always aim higher
- Remain calm and composed
- Take criticism and mistakes well
- Take necessary risks

- Believe in their skills and abilities

WHAT IF A LEADER DOESN'T HAVE SELF-CONFIDENCE AND SELF-TRUST?

If a leader lacks confidence, it can have a negative impact on their leadership style and its efficacy. A leader may then:

- They find it difficult to praise others, so they struggle to motivate their team members.
- Have a tendency to take all the credit, which can again demotivate their team members who have diligently worked towards a common goal. It can also cause conflict and unhappiness within the team.
- Keep important information to themselves, which can destroy trust and communication between team members.
- Criticizing others regularly and having a constant negative attitude like this can impact the atmosphere in the whole workplace and the team.
- Micromanage gives the team members the impression they aren't trusted to carry out tasks.
- Being indecisive shows a lack of confidence in themselves and their abilities.
- Be arrogant. Arrogance is not confidence. Remember, you have to lead by example, and

there's always something to be learned from every situation. Being able to accept feedback and learn lessons when things don't work shows that you're human and that you're not afraid of challenges and change.

11 TIPS FOR DEVELOPING LEADERSHIP CONFIDENCE

You've already started developing your leadership confidence by working through this book. If you want to keep going, here are some useful tips:

- Learn about leadership
- Celebrate your wins and encourage others to do the same
- Network and collaborate with other leaders
- Support others so that they can be successful too
- Develop realistic self-awareness
- Learn and practice gratitude and positive psychology
- Look confident, and project that confidence
- Develop your emotional intelligence
- Don't be afraid to ask for help
- Stop asking 'Mother, may I' and make your decision
- Develop your sense of humor

Remember, building the trust and confidence you

feel for yourself is just one part of your journey to becoming a great early leader. The next part of your journey is focused on building your credibility and developing your ability to influence others. You can only do that if you believe in yourself and your abilities. Once you've nailed this then, others will see you as the leader you are, trust you, and follow you.

Your Practice Opportunity

Self-confidence isn't something that just appears overnight. The best way to develop it is to build your daily routine around it. By making it your top priority, you'll be ready for the day ahead before you even get to work. You can do many things to build your confidence, and it will develop with practice. If you're unsure where to start, use our daily Self-Confidence Routine Builder below.

1. Focus on your strengths even in times of difficulty.

Make a quick list of your strengths and the things you're most proud of. Print it out or store it on your cell phone. Look at it as many times per day as you need to.
   a.   Strength 1 ...
   b.   Strength 2 ...
   c.   Strength 3 ...
   d.   Strength 4 ...
   e.   I'm proud of ...

    f.   I'm proud of ...
    g.   I'm proud of ...
    h.   I'm proud of ...

2. Reward yourself for the positive steps you made in the right direction.

This can be a simple "well done" or a quick run to Starbucks for a great latte. These are small gestures of congratulations and appreciation we tend never to take the time to do for ourselves.

3. Slow down

Think of the situation that's holding you back or preventing you from taking the steps you'd like to move forward. Think logically through the situation and see what steps you could take to solve the problem/challenge. Visualize what that would look and feel like. If it feels good on all counts, go ahead, and take the first step.

4. Express your feelings and needs

People struggling with self-confidence issues tend to become the "yes person" at work. If everyone knows that you are that person, it will become easier for you to be taken advantage of. Instead, think about your workload and see if saying "yes" will add unnecessary additional work, putting you behind. It's ok to say "no."

5. The START-STOP-CONTINUE method

Use this method to figure out what you need to stop doing, which does not serve you anymore, start doing because it's good for you, and continue doing because it works.

a. **START** taking small breaks every hour so that I can relax my eyes and my mind between tasks.

b. **STOP** constantly saying "yes" to everything. It puts me behind in my work.

c. **CONTINUE** to plan my day and block time on my calendar to catch up on work and other tasks.

GAINING CREDIBILITY AND INFLUENCING OTHERS

*B*uilding credibility and influencing others is just as important once you've developed confidence in yourself. When you believe in yourself, others start to believe in you. With every success or win, you start to build credibility, and—eventually—you'll start to influence better.

Being credible means showing others they can trust you. Proving yourself credible in the business world is extremely important as this helps cultivate a positive image of yourself as a leader and authority figure. As you do this, you will be able to use your skills to influence your direct reports and encourage them to ensure the organization as a whole can influence the business world and its customers.

A leader with credibility becomes known—in the organization—as someone everyone can trust. If you are known for getting things done, breaking down barriers, and motivating or inspiring others, you will become an influential figure. Building your credibility and being able to influence will allow you to become a seasoned leader in no time. Your reputation will precede you. People will come to you to tap into your expertise and dynamic thinking abilities.

When customers buy a product or service, they often buy from the people they trust. They don't simply buy the product or service. They buy the vision. If you show others you are invested in the business and believe in yourself, you will inspire your direct reports to do the same. It's your passion and beliefs that will drive them. To gain credibility, there are 3 strategies you can use. We're going to begin by covering those. Then we'll explore further ways to build credibility and then focus on your leadership powers and how they can help you influence others.

To be an influential leader, you have to deliver what you say you will, to agreed deadlines, and in a way that helps and supports your people. It's time to take your leadership development to a whole new level—now you've already begun building confidence in yourself, it's time to gain credibility from others as well...

THREE STRATEGIES TO CULTIVATE YOUR CREDIBILITY

Developing your credibility as a young leader is a challenge, but thankfully there are three easy ways in which this can be done:

1. Grow your skills

Being a leader is a huge responsibility, and it's up to you to develop the necessary skills to help your team and organization reach their goals successfully. Develop a plan to grow your skills in leading, communicating, and dealing with conflict. You also have to think about any other specific skills you will need to inspire, motivate, and organize your team. Make your team believe in you by showing them the way. They will not always believe what you say, but to be effective, they need to believe what you do!

2. Be a leader that's worth following

Really consider other successful leaders and what characteristics make them that way. Your direct reports will follow you if you have integrity, are trustworthy, and project confidence. They also want you to be passionate and positive about your work so that you inspire and spark their motivation when you show up. Nobody enjoys having a negative leader who is ineffective in problem-solving.

3. Develop successful leadership habits

A successful leader develops positive habits to improve their performance. If you have solid habits, you are twice as likely to achieve your goals, and this also allows you to embrace consistency (another good habit). For example, if you focus on your strengths and the strengths of your team—and you use them in a complementary way to effectively work together—you can build good teamwork habits.

Although others will instantly have a first impression of you, trust isn't built overnight. It takes time, practice, and patience. That's why it's important to start building your credibility now. But sometimes, it's difficult to know where to begin.

BUILDING YOUR CREDIBILITY WHEN YOU'RE A NEW LEADER

If building credibility is important to you as a new leader, there are some skills you can work on right away. Being consistent is key. For example, trust is built faster when you show up, manage your direct reports, and problem-solve consistently. You can also utilize your listening skills in a way that shows your direct reports that you care. As a leader, it is always good to attentively listen to others first before you jump in and offer advice or guidance. Your team may simply need someone to talk to or share their ideas with, and providing a listening ear can be more effective than you realize.

Another important leadership skill is getting to know the teams you will collaborate with. Here I am referring to your direct reports, the management team, and other business teams closely linked to your and your clients. Trust often comes naturally when you know the people you will work closely with, and they know you. Such relationships are vital to maintaining and finding your sponsors when an occasion calls for it!

When it comes to the business world, we have no time to waste. So, be direct and get straight to the point! Maintaining professionalism and politeness is important, but being direct gives the impression of honesty. Respond to others clearly, simply, and succinctly to ensure that you clearly express your goals and priorities. People appreciate honesty, and it builds both respect and trust.

As a leader, it's up to you to take action. Put your trust in training and education. Development is crucial for you to become a better leader. Most corporate training is highly valuable, and regardless of whether you are a new or experienced leader, training and education will ensure you continuously develop and grow, so invest your time and energy in it. While it is likely it will improve performance in the long term, it's unlikely that opportunities will find you. Take responsibility, and seek out speaking opportunities. They will help enhance your visibility and reputation and ensure you are known for your expertise.

Your growth will become evident if you diligently work on improving your skills. Influencing others will happen naturally by cultivating your credibility as a new, innovative, and dynamic leader.

USING YOUR LEADERSHIP POWERS TO INFLUENCE OTHERS

As a leader, you have the power to influence others. *But what is power?* It's the capacity or ability to influence events or people. A leadership role grants you the power to lead a team, but it also provides you with many responsibilities. All good leaders can encourage self-improvement within their team and embrace team-work, as well as have the power to promote a positive team culture. It's your job to influence others; you just have to tap into the types of power that allow you to do this.

What 'powers' do leaders have or can use?

As a leader, you will recognize some of the powers. You will likely find that you already have and use some of these powers when influencing others. Many people find they have influence through their connections, such as being associated with an influential person who is already admired and respected by others. That will give them power by association. For example, if the organization you work for is looking for an investor and you know possible suitable investors, you can leverage those connections. Many people find power through their value system. If you passionately believe in something and are known for doing so, it may inspire others to take positive action as they strongly believe in the same thing as you. It's easier to influence others if they believe in similar things as you. Common ground is powerful.

Your role within an organization—and the respect others have for you—can also legitimize and position you as an authority figure. Founders who are leaders are often respected due to their experience within the business, as a result of the links they have to the organization since its birth. This respect gives them power, as everyone knows their status within the organization. Often leaders who are recognized as experts in a particular area can easily influence others as they frequently become the 'go-to' person.

Some of the powers you have as a leader are linked to your powers of persuasion. If you have charisma, you can compel others to follow you because you inspire positivity and happiness within them. There's just something about you that makes people want to follow you. Rewards are another way to persuade your direct reports to perform. Leaders often have the power to grant incentives or other rewards, which will encourage employees to complete tasks and exceed expectations. A leader with strong interpersonal skills may also find that others admire them and follow them naturally. Having knowledge and information about the organization that others do not also puts you in a unique, powerful position as a leader. Knowing something before others do indicates that you are an authority figure within the company.

Being aware of the powers you have as a leader allows you to harness them. You can use these powers to help others succeed.

Your Practice Opportunity

It's your turn to build your credibility, as this is one

of the most important aspects of becoming a great leader. Building connections through trust will allow you to grow and develop your brand as the 'go-to' person. This, in turn, will increase your visibility within the organization.

Can I Trust You?

Idea: Build Connections

Build connections at work. Folks you can count on for advice. The more connections you can make, the more people you can reach out to for support when you need it most. Building connections is about building trust. The more others trust you, the more credible you will become to them. This takes time and effort on your part. Fostering relationships in the workplace will become one of the most important skills you can learn.

Goal: Be Reliable

People trust those they can count on. Once they believe you are trustworthy, you will become reliable in their eyes. Reliability is crucial to your success as a leader. Make that your brand, and you will never have to worry about your growth within your organization.

Ideas of How to Build Connections

1. Join committees

2. Become a mentor to newer employees
3. Attend social events

Score yourself from 1 to 10 on the following questions:

- How reliable am I right now?
- How good are my current connections?
- How trustworthy am I right now?

If you have scored five or less on any of the above, examine where you need to focus more of your time. Find ways to increase your trust factor.

Can I Respect You?

Idea: Play Big

Create a list of achievements and accomplishments and find a way to speak about them in a way that feels authentic to you. This is not the time to downplay your skills, education, and experience. Showcase what you know in a way that works for you. Success is a great thing, and it should be appreciated and expressed. You worked hard to get there and need to let them know.

Goal: Be Humble

There is no better way to self-promote than by others promoting you. You can accomplish this by adding value via sharing information on the content you published, or your expertise on a topic, or simply by becoming a thought expert. This will establish you as a professional in your field. Your colleagues will reciprocate by willingly promoting your expertise.

4

SPEAKING UP – GAINING VISIBILITY

*A*s a leader, you'll often be expected to step out of your comfort zone and confront your fears. One of the most common reasons people feel uncomfortable when they are gaining visibility is because putting themselves out there is scary! But look, it's a MUST. The most effective way to gain visibility is to speak publicly.

Have you ever heard the saying, feeding yourself to the wolves? Well, when you're highly visible, it can often feel like you're exposing yourself to what you perceive as dangerous since you are opening yourself up to judgment. Of course, there will always be people out there who cast their judgments on you regardless. But being visible isn't always as bad as we believe it will be; we simply frighten ourselves with anticipation. Research tells us that **99% of the things we worry about never happen.**

It's been estimated that approximately 75% of people are intimidated by public speaking. This is an interesting figure when you consider that we are always doing some type of public speaking! We speak publicly when we email or talk on the phone. When we participate in meetings or bump into someone in the hallway. Every single time we communicate with others, we present ourselves in a way that impacts how we are perceived. That's because communication allows others to form an impression of us.

Visibility is something you have to work on. To make this a seamless exercise, this chapter is divided into three parts:

1. Prepare
2. Practice
3. Present

Each of these parts plays a crucial role in increasing your visibility. By the end of this chapter, you will have a better idea of what you can do as a leader when you sign-up for high-visibility projects, and you'll understand how this can strengthen your team's trust.

Preparation is key if you want to gain visibility. Being prepared removes some of the fear and anxiety we feel about being visible. To prepare effectively, you can:

Pick me!

- It's time to be proactive by creating and finding opportunities
- Be receptive and open by saying 'yes' to the opportunities offered to you

Who are you addressing?

- Take your time researching your audience, or at least have a good idea of who they are. Everyone needs to know this so that they can tailor the way they present. Don't be afraid to challenge their assumptions either – this will make you memorable
- Tailor your speaking points to your audience. Once you know whom you're speaking to, think about what they need to know and make them part of your plan when thinking about your points for discussion

Who's on your side, and whose side are you on?

- Inspire others and encourage them to use their voice with confidence
- Offer opportunities to help others find their voice! Building these connections can help others. If you go the extra mile to help them, they'll likely reciprocate and treat you the same way. This is called reciprocity

Preparing allows you to plan your public speaking

and be ready for anything coming your way. Once you've planned it, it's time to practice.

PRACTICE CHECKLIST

If you needed to make a speech to your family at a special event, you'd probably write it down and practice… right? Practicing for a public speaking event should be handled similarly and can build your confidence. The steps are:

Stretch, challenge, and contribute

- Consider how you use your voice. When do you speak up? When do you hold back? Reflect on these things to improve your practice
- Provide feedback in a clear and honest way. You'll find that others appreciate this

Practice, practice, and practice some more

- Practice by presenting to your family, friends, allies, and kids, in front of the mirror, in front of a video recorder, or even to your pets!
- Every time you do, work on something you'd like to improve

- Put everything into your presentation—your mind, body, heart, and voice are all important. People want to hear the real you!
- Encourage others to practice by offering to be a test audience member for them

Center yourself, and don't let your nerves become a problem

Develop your ritual or mantra to help you stay calm, focused, and ready.

Remember to breathe. If you find your breathing changes, close your eyes, inhale deeply, and push out your breath from the pit of your stomach.

Stay in the present moment. Try not to think about tomorrow or yesterday; enjoy the experience in-the-now

PRESENTATION CHECKLIST

When you present, you can use different methods to communicate effectively. You can show your passion when you present through more than just your voice— your hand gestures and tone of voice also make an impression on others. Presenting can help you build your confidence and credibility and give you a platform from which to influence. And remember, as we've already covered, this skill can be strengthened. When you're ready to present, you need to:

Communicate clearly and expressively

- Pace your speech so your audience can follow and engage with it. Use pauses to allow your audience to process what you've just told them, go slower when you tell them something important, and speed up (not too much) if you say something lighthearted or funny. Try to connect with your audience and gauge their understanding and enjoyment of your talk.

- Consider your pitch. Your pitch tells your audience about you and your energy levels. We've already mentioned the tone of voice and how you can use it to convey your mood. Try also to remain conscious of your inflection so that you can use it to check in with your audience; it tells you how engaged they are. If you get nervous, breathe deeply to tap into your deeper vocal tones and reduce your pitch. Remember the feeling of being confident and in control.

- Consider your projection. *Whom do you need to reach? What feeling or action do you want to evoke?* Your projection helps you to harmonize with your energy and center. Show feelings in your speech—for example, speak low and lean in for serious points, or raise your voice to increase your energy levels or enthusiasm. You can use it to add emphasis to your points! Always remember that the farthest person away from you is listening. Obviously, you want them to hear you. So, do your best to speak so that they can, and finally, use a microphone if necessary.

Non-verbal communication

- Facial expressions can be used to add feelings to your talk. Smiling shows you are warm. In return, the audience can and will show whether they like something through their expressions. More than half of a presenter's message is communicated through non-verbal cues. That's how powerful it is!
- Posture shows your energy levels, so pay attention to it. If you stand or sit up straight, with your shoulders back, you'll look confident and approachable. Your posture can help you appear strong and cultivate presence.
- Gestures are also great for displaying confidence and strengthening presence. If you shrug when you don't know or wave when you say 'hello,' it shows increased energy when you're presenting.
- Eye contact communicates integrity and fosters trust. If you want your audience to believe you, engage with you, and trust you,

you will need to make eye contact. Whereas, if you look at the floor and fidget, you'll appear less believable. Eye contact shows boldness and confidence in what you are sharing.

- Your appearance also shapes people's impressions of you. As a young leader and presenter, show up ready. That means dressing professionally, and considering the event's formality, as this will help you decide what type of clothing you need to wear, but always honor your uniqueness. We are not all the same. Wear something that fills you with confidence and is appropriate for the occasion!

Organize your thoughts by thinking in threes.

- Thinking in threes allows you structure and encourages you to think on your feet. If you embed this strategy in your mind, it will ensure you can speak about anything in-the-moment. We will speak more about this in the coming chapters.
- Offer a Q&A at the end of the session. Tell them what you would do first of all… then second… then finally. Chances are that you'll be surprised by what you come up with, as it's much more effective than simply giving one answer to a question. A Q&A shows that

you are not afraid to be put on the spot by your audience, which adds to your presence and integrity. If you don't have an answer, simply tell the person you'll find out and get back to them. Practice summarizing your thoughts, and consider different perspectives or approaches in relation to your topic. This can be a great way to feel more prepared for any curve balls

Your Practice Opportunity

The best thing to improve your visibility is to practice your presentation skills. This plays an integral role in feeling more comfortable when presenting.

> *"Practice makes comfort. Expand your experiences regularly so every stretch won't feel like your first."*
> ~ Gina Greenlee

There is no better way to become super proficient at presenting than practice every time you have an opportunity. Now, it's your opportunity to practice, so use the following tip sheet to help you prepare for your next presentation.

SPEAKING & PRESENTING PREP LIST

SPEAKING/PRESENTING PREP LIST

VOCAL COMMUNICATION

PACE – Drives the ENERGY of the audience
• How is my pace? Too slow, too fast, or just right?
PITCH – Communicates the state of your own ENERGY
• How do I communicate with those I care about? Do I feel comfortable?
PROJECTION – Helps to harmonize my ENERGY with that of the audience
• Raise your voice to emphasize. Lower your voice to relax the audience

NON-VERBAL COMMUNICATION

Facial Expressions – Adjust your expressions to what you are saying
Posture – Power postures work to build confidence and project your voice
Gestures – Match your gestures to your speech. Rest your hand to pause
Eye Contact – Look to the Left, to the Middle, to the Right of the room
Appearance/Clothing – Look professional, feel more confident

THINK IN THREES

Give yourself structure with the rule of 3's:
The first thing I would say is ...
The second thing is ...
Thirdly ...

Q & A

This shows the audience that you have total command of the room
What questions do you have?
How did you do this differently?
Who else has a perfective on this?
What worked for you? What didn't?

5

INFLUENCING UP – HOW TO DO THIS THE RIGHT WAY?

*W*e've talked about influence already, but we're going to revisit it now because— especially as an early-career leader—it is extremely important. If influencing is important to you, earning respect and credibility is key. There is often an assumption that leaders are older and more experienced folks. If this assumption is true, then this would mean that the young leader is at risk of not being taken seriously. Increasing your influence levels can stop this assumption and demonstrate that a young leader should never be underestimated!

When we talk about increasing influence in leadership, we notice that many new managers don't know how to make that happen successfully and where to start. First and foremost, you might have to break down barriers and beliefs your direct reports may have when it comes to following young leaders. This chapter focuses on how you can do this correctly to ensure you build influence as quickly as possible, not just within your team but within your organization.

WHAT DOES LEADERSHIP LOOK LIKE FOR A YOUNG LEADER?

It's refreshing to see young leaders within organizations, but they often face many unique hurdles. The idea that leaders are typically over thirty-five or older means that there are often differences in work ethic, communication styles, and priorities between the younger and older generations. As a result, many young leaders find it challenging to gain respect and influence in the workplace from older staff members. There are ways to overcome this.

Young or early-career leaders often bring vibrant and creative ways of thinking, a fresh new approach to things, and unique perspectives to the business. They are hired because the organization believes they can do their job well, but team members can find it difficult to settle under a young leader with these new ideas. Everyone must adapt to change, but it's up to you as a leader to help your direct reports rise to the challenge. If an organization is looking to move forward and improve its performance, the energy a young leader brings can be the catalyst that makes it happen.

The generation gap is increasing as older generations delay their retirement while more college graduates are hired into leadership roles despite having less experience. This doesn't mean that young leaders are not right for the role; it simply means they need to adapt, learn, and grow as they settle into their roles. Gaining influence is one way you can do this.

But how can young leaders gain the influence they need to lead their teams well and earn the respect they deserve?

You need to help them form a positive opinion of you!

GAINING INFLUENCE AS A YOUNG LEADER

If you want to gain influence, you need to develop your communication skills, build strong relationships with your team members, and ensure you are clear on the goals of both the business and the individuals involved. Take responsibility by showing you are interested in your team and its dynamics. You must have a strong understanding of the goals and pressures faced by employees, regardless of age gaps. Both individual and organizational goals should align with each other, and it's up to you to ensure they do. Make sure you are clear on all business goals, mission statements, and values so you can support your team and align them with the requirements of your organization and its structure. Alignment is key to ensuring you are all on the same page. You must gauge your direct reports' knowledge, strengths, and potential gaps in those areas, as this can help you delegate tasks and give stretch assignments effectively. Remember, you're setting your team up to win if you give them tasks that play to their strengths and help them stretch and develop in the process!

As an emerging leader, how you communicate makes a big difference. Working closely with your team, informing them how you like to receive information, and considering their preferences are really important. Understanding each person's preferred communication style can make your job easier. Your direct reports are also interested in how you deal with conflict, so ensure you have a good listening ear and are ready to problem-solve when conflict arises. Be open and honest when you inform them of how to communicate or approach you. Showing you are willing to listen and resolve any issues in this way will help you gain their respect and trust. This will begin to strengthen relationships within your team as well. Communication is such an important aspect of business, so take your time in the beginning, to learn what works and what doesn't so that you can succeed in the long run.

While this helps you gain respect and build influence in the workplace, you can take it further by working on your relationships with your direct reports. Obviously, your life will be easier if you have positive relationships with team members! Also, if team members are happy, productivity and job satisfaction increase. Team meetings, one-to-one meetings with your direct reports, or team/social activities are great ways to strengthen relationships. To install a sense of teamwork, you can increase your credibility by ensuring you understand exactly who you want to influence. Then, build your relationships individually using what you know about your direct reports.

Gaining credibility with your customers can be achieved through a similar process as with your direct reports. A leader who has influence always remains client-focused, can deliver on their word and has a deep understanding of what value they bring to the table. Your client will then trust you and, by extension, the organization as a whole. A leader who has credibility outside the business, in light of the work they do for the organization, has the power to influence.

Your Practice Opportunity

Before you start influencing others, it's a good idea to find out your influencing style. Do you push or pull? Let's test your influencing style with the questionnaire below.

Influencing Style Questionnaire

Please read each of the following statements carefully and decide the extent to which they describe your behavior in situations where you need to influence others. Base your answers on typical day-to-day activities which occur in your job.

Please be as frank as possible. The questionnaire

will be of little value unless you provide an accurate and objective description of your behavior.

Against each statement, enter the score that corresponds to your choice from the five possible responses below in the appropriate box.

Enter the score:

4 - if you definitely agree, that is if the statement accurately describes your actions

3 - if you are inclined to agree, that is, if the statement describes your actions with reasonable accuracy

2 - if you are undecided, that is, you are genuinely unsure whether or not the statement describes your actions accurately

1 - if you are inclined to disagree, that is, if you think the statement probably does not describe your actions accurately

0 - if you definitely disagree, that is, if the statement definitely does not describe your actions

Please answer the questionnaire as quickly as possible, and don't hesitate to use the extreme score where appropriate.

Influencing Style Questionnaire

Please read each of the following statements carefully and decide the extent to which they describe your behaviour in situations where you need to influence others. Base your answers on typical day-to-day activities which occur in your job.

Please be as frank as possible. The questionnaire will be of little value unless you provide an accurate and objective description of your behaviour.

Against each statement, enter in the appropriate box the score which corresponds to your choice from the five possible responses below.

Enter the score:

4   if you definite agree, that is, if the statement accurately describes your actions

3   if you are inclined to agree, that is, if the statement describes your actions with reasonable accuracy

2   if you are undecided, that is, you are genuinely unsure whether or not the statement describes your actions accurately

1   if you are inclined to disagree, that is, if you think the statement probably does not describe your actions accurately

0   if you definitely disagree, that is, if the statement definitely does not describe your actions

Please answer the questionnaire as quickly as possible and don' t hesitate to use the extreme score where appropriate.

6

HOW TO EFFECTIVELY COMMUNICATE WITH YOUR TEAM

*W*hile we've provided insight into communication throughout the previous chapters, it's especially important for emerging leaders to recognize how essential effective communication with your team really is. Let me ask you this, *how can you expect your team to work effectively and meet high-performance targets if you can't communicate what you expect of them?*

> "*In teamwork, silence isn't golden; it's deadly.*"
> ~ Mark Sanborn

As the quote suggests, more is better for your team: More communication, openness to listening and providing feedback, and clarity. A lack of communication can be deadly to your team. Chapter 5 talked about young leaders having to lead multiple generations of people. As an emerging leader, you must perfect your communication skills to have more impact. Enhancing your communication is an important step towards successfully leading your team.

Many young leaders find it challenging to maintain respect and authority when managing employees older than themselves. This chapter will focus on a few simple steps to improve your communication skills while exerting your authority. It's time for you to learn to communicate with courage and confidence!

WHY IS IT SO DAUNTING FOR A YOUNG LEADER TO LEAD OLDER GENERATIONS?

If we're going to resolve this problem, it's important to understand why the problem arose in the first place. To a young manager, older employees often appear intimidating for three reasons:

1. The older employee has many years of work experience, which may include several with the company you're now working for.
2. It takes more time for the older, more experienced employee to trust their new, younger leader fully. They at least want to see some proof that you know what you are doing.
3. It can be uncomfortable for you as a younger leader to give direction to an older, more

experienced employee, especially if you are new to leadership.

Newsflash! If you want to lead, you must be willing to get uncomfortable!

Yes, older employees may have many more years of working experience in this or another organization. But your experience is different from theirs and just as valuable. You have a lot to offer, and you worked hard to get to this point in your career. Your expertise is in leading others, or at least it will be once you are done reading this book. Therefore, when you become a leader who is an expert in managing people, and your team comprises employees from older generations with lots of experience, you can do great things together!

If an older employee is unwilling to respect you, then this says more about their character than yours as a leader. Sometimes it takes time to earn your team's respect. Good leaders understand this and take time to learn about the team they will lead. If this is the case for your team, then don't take it personally! Unwillingness is often a response based on their dysfunctional beliefs or fears—you can change their mind by showing them respect and leading well.

That's right. You can lead older generations and be respected at the same time. Don't forget that respect is a two-way street; there is no room for disrespect in the workplace. You will eventually earn your team's respect if you communicate well and demonstrate confidence in your abilities. Be patient and remain consistent in your approach.

I hope this gives you an insight into why leading older generations can be challenging but not impossible. It's important to be consistent in your role as a leader. Consistency brings about trust, and trust creates super-teams!

HOW TO MANAGE COMMUNICATION EFFECTIVELY AS A YOUNG EMERGING LEADER

As a leader, you must be able to manage communication effectively. You can do this by:

Not wasting time on assumptions

Don't waste your time on the assumptions you make... or the assumptions you believe others make about you. Be direct, honest, polite, and respectful, and ensure you know the facts before you form opinions. Getting to know your team

—and the business you're working for—will help make this happen. Again, don't dwell on assumptions others may make about you; simply focus on performing to the best of your ability, and you will change their minds with your work ethic!

Be mindful of tradition

Sometimes, there are traditions in a workplace that

are important to the employees who have worked there for a long time. Be mindful of these and get involved. Suppose you try to alter a tradition that's important to your team members. In that case, it could cause conflict, so try to understand and respect traditions by leaving them in place unless it's necessary to change.

Don't command and demand—instead, make an effort to understand

If you start leading your team by barking orders, making demands, and commanding your direct reports, your team will not perform in a productive way. There's so much more to being a leader than showing them who's the boss. You need to inspire, motivate, and empathize with your team. Take time to communicate by talking things through and getting to know them. Allow team discussions to occur if new projects are coming up, conflicts are occurring, or targets are not being met. Creating an inclusive environment where every opinion counts can increase morale within the team.

Don't be distracted by age

Age is just a number! So don't let it distract you from doing your job. If you are finding it difficult to deal with an older direct report, remember you have a duty to treat them in the same way as your other direct reports. While you may approach them differently, you still need to be direct and honest. You deserve to be in your leadership role, regardless of age.

Recognize generational preferences

We all work in different ways, and it's important to recognize this. As a leader, you must recognize generational preferences and be flexible when necessary. While you could simply exert your authority, working with your team members will allow you to build relationships and will show that you're adaptable. For example, if your team member prefers quick calls over exchanging emails because they value discussing in person, try to accommodate their communication style. It's important to recognize that generational differences like this do exist, and they aren't a bad thing. In this example, a quick phone call can resolve what emails might take all day in five minutes. A lot of time can be wasted on the back-and-forth, whereas a quick conversation will resolve the issue instantly.

Effectively communicating with your team should be important to all leaders. However, you're still trying to build your credibility and gain respect from your team, so *how do you manage others' perceptions of you?* Let's talk about this in chapter 7!

7

HOW TO MANAGE THEIR PERCEPTION OF YOU

*Y*ou are probably familiar with the phrase, "perception is reality," *but have you ever considered what this really means?*

Perception is the result of understanding and interpreting something. In other words, it's other people's interpretation of your behavior based on their belief system. It will be the things they believe to be true. What does that mean for you? It means people will assess your abilities and your effectiveness all the time. They will observe what you do, which will impact their reality and beliefs about you— this will create their perception of you.

Perception is individualized, but often things aren't what they appear to be. One event can have many different interpretations. That's why this chapter focuses on how leaders can manage perceptions.

THE MANY INTERPRETATIONS OF A SINGLE EVENT

People often interpret events in different ways. Let's consider the fable below:

A farmer once had one horse, and that horse ran away. His neighbors consoled him, expecting him to be angry and sad. The farmer simply said, "We'll see. Who can know what's good and what's bad?"

The next week, the horse returned and brought dozens of wild horses with it. He and his son rounded them all up. His neighbors commented on his good fortune. They expected him to be happy, but again the farmer said, "We'll see. Who can know what's good and what's bad?"

The next day, one of the new horses broke the farmer's son's legs by trampling him. His neighbors said they were sorry. They expected him to be upset, but once more, the farmer said, "We'll see. Who can know what's good and what's bad?"

Not long after, the country was at war. They drafted every young, healthy man into the military to fight. As he was injured, the farmer's son was not called upon. During this terrible war, almost every soldier died. The farmer's neighbors congratulated him on his son not going to war. They expected him to be happy and relieved, but the father's response stayed the same. "We'll see. Who can know what's good and what's bad?"

What's the moral of that story? Perception is not always right, but it sure can feel very real. The events his neighbors viewed as bad influenced other events that resulted in something positive. The horse returned with other horses at the story's start, which was great for the farmer. Sometimes positive events result in something bad happening, like how the other horses then trampled the farmer's boy. Who are we to really know whether something is good or bad? Things just happen!

Your interpretation of life and its events often dictates how you feel. The neighbors in the story quickly judge the situation the farmer experiences, yet he is careful not to get swept up in those judgments. He understands that there are multiple interpretations for every event in life. Just like him, you get to choose how you feel about things. You are in control of your own narrative.

This whole concept helps you understand your mind's impact and how it is shaped by everything in life that you experience.

HOW MANAGING PERCEPTIONS SETS YOU APART FROM OTHER LEADERS

Do you know how to use your ability to manage perceptions to set yourself apart from other leaders? One of the ways you can do this is by controlling your own narrative. This is one of the greatest skills to develop, and it will help you as a leader and person. By choosing what path to take, you take back control. This can be empowering, as you are not allowing your energy to be controlled by random events, which frees you up to choose something that increases your energy levels. Controlling the narrative shows your confidence and demonstrates your boldness. Others will recognize this in you.

When you control the narrative, you have the ability to choose the most empowering one for you. Of course, this has to be a truthful narrative. No good comes from burying your head in the sand and refusing to believe the truth! The same is true of ignoring negative events because you want to promote positive thinking. It's about dealing with events, understanding that the narrative is not fixed, and realizing that your perspective determines your experience. You always have command of your perspective!

There are challenges you will face when controlling your narrative. The main issue faced by young leaders who have attempted to do this is the fact that our brains process perceptions automatically. That means controlling your narrative takes practice, as you have to reprogram your mind to interpret things differently. It will take time and effort, but being mindful can play a key role in altering what you decide to see. Once you consciously change your mind about what you choose to see—and how—you will begin to notice your automatic responses and prevent your initial reaction from happening instantaneously. Being more aware allows you to gain control.

HOW TO MANAGE PERCEPTIONS

How people perceive you as a leader is important. Unmanaged perceptions become rumors, which turn to gossip, and then an untruthful story is formed. This can be destructive for your working environment, so it's important you manage the perceptions of others. *But how do you manage other people's perceptions of you?*

If your goal is to influence, lead, and communicate well with others, the first step is to understand how others perceive you so that you can remedy any perceptions that don't align with who you really are. You can accomplish this by:

Getting feedback from others—by asking for feedback, you invite others to share how they perceive you. You can then spend some time in self-reflection, considering what feedback you received. Being willing to analyze the feedback takes commitment and courage, but success will follow if you are willing to be open.

Follow through on what you say—this will allow you to motivate your team and act with conviction. Your actions must match your words. It's best to communicate the reasons behind your decisions and do so continuously. Give them the 'why' behind the 'what.' You must also follow through with your actions and show that others can trust you and take you at your word. If you don't, you will leave much room for interpretation, and they may perceive you as untrustworthy.

Be aware of how you impact others—as a leader, you need to be aware of the impact stress has on you and how this appears to others. Be visible during tough and good times to answer questions, have discussions, or celebrate with your team. Show up as the leader at all times and allow your direct reports to see you! *Seeing is believing*, as they say.

As obvious as this may sound, it is worth stating—if people do not perceive you as their leader, they will not follow you. They will likely choose to leave, adding extra stress and hiring costs. It will also impact the effectiveness and performance of your team. So, ensuring you are perceived in the right way—as early as possible is key— poor perceptions stick like mud and are much more difficult to alter later.

OK, before we had to section II, stop what you are doing right now, please! Are you enjoying this book? Are you getting value from it for yourself? *If you answered 'Yes' to both questions, please take 2 minutes of your time, and leave me your honest feedback. Scan or click on the QR code below.* You will help many other amazing, new female leaders decide to buy this book and learn how to make a difference truly. Your feedback can make that happen. So, don't wait; post your feedback now; even if you just give it 5 stars, that's enough for someone to choose this book and make a career-changing decision.

SECTION II – LEADING INDIVIDUALS

As a leader, you clearly have a responsibility to manage others. A part of your role is to keep them engaged and motivated. While leading yourself is important, you must also lead your direct reports. Often people are disengaged due to a lack of effective leadership.

Remember...

"You don't inspire your teammates by showing them how amazing you are; you inspire them by showing them how amazing they are."
~ Robyn Benincase

This section focuses on leading individuals in the most effective way, so you can motivate and encourage them to perform at their best. You will explore how you can become a better leader by leading human beings, understanding the importance of authenticity, and studying key strategies that allow you to provide feedback to your direct reports in the most impactful way.

You'll have the opportunity to develop your leadership skills further by analyzing communication strategies and improving the psychological safety of your staff. We'll also cover how you can implement motivation tactics by recognizing and spotlighting and then perfecting your ability to delegate as a leader.

Leading individuals is an opportunity for a great leader to help others grow. Your ability to lead your direct reports well can improve your team and the workplace culture.

Let's explore this first...

8

HOW TO LEAD HUMAN BEINGS

*O*ur employees are human beings, and it's important that we don't lose sight of that as leaders. In this chapter, you will discover how you can lead human beings by considering the hopes and dreams of your direct reports and their fears and concerns. Each of these is an essential part of human nature, and—to lead well—an effective leader needs to incorporate their humanness into their leadership style.

We will also explore your humanness as a leader so that you can build strong, lasting connections with your team and the other people that make up your organization.

In our ultra-connected world, paradoxically, we often find ourselves less connected than ever. Our leaders are responsible for fostering and embracing connections within our team. Increasing human connection will make the business even more successful and increase performance!

WHAT CAN 'HUMANNESS' BRING TO MY LEADERSHIP STYLE?

As a leader, there are five key ways you can bring humanness into your leadership style:

1. You are human, and it's important that you show this side of yourself when leading. Your team needs to see the real you. Yes, that includes your flaws. Being ourselves comes naturally to us, and this makes us approachable. Your experience helps you develop your leadership style. So, by opening up, you're prompting others to do the same, boosting human connection.

2. Be self-aware. We talked about self-awareness earlier in this book. Taking the time to reflect and become aware of what we're good at—or not so good at—is a positive thing. Many people don't consider why we do things or say the things we say, but this is certainly something we need to reflect on to become more self-aware. By doing regular self-check-ins, we can lead with compassion and empathy, which means we'll build human connections along the way.

3. Understand others. Sometimes people behave in a particular way, and we simply don't 'get it.' But if you want to bring humanness into your leadership style, you must at least try. Focus on who they are rather than what they do, and appreciate them. Be compassionate towards them so they know you care and can trust you. Remember to include your team members in discussions about work topics and find out what they think. Promoting inclusivity and soliciting feedback from them can help you understand them better and improve human connection.

4. Be polite! Being a leader doesn't excuse you from being kind, courteous, and polite to others. It's often an expectation we have of others, showing that we appreciate others. A simple 'thank you' can make our direct reports feel so much better about the work they have done.

5. Be a visible and accessible leader. Traditionally, leaders and managers were not seen very often. Those days are gone. So, if you expect your team to communicate and perform well, you must be seen, and your team must feel able to approach you. You can use your human connection to build a happy and productive team.

An old proverb suggests that to be a great leader,

you first must become a good human being. This has never been truer than it is now! If we connect with others and embrace our human side, we will raise other achievers and leaders because they will feel able to accomplish anything.

Incorporating humanness into the way you lead has many benefits, so let's explore this before we close this chapter.

WHAT ARE THE BENEFITS OF ADOPTING HUMANNESS WHEN LEADING OTHERS?

Traditionally, leaders and managers have led their teams through appraisal or fear, but today's leaders have a more well-rounded perspective. Modern leaders are known for their creativity, innovation, and ability to enable others. Such leaders have several benefits for the organization.

1. The ultimate benefit of adopting humanness when leading is that it drives employee engagement. This means staff is more productive in their work, as they are fully invested in their work. This way, the business attracts the best candidates. It means the right person has the right skills to do their job and can bring a fresh approach with them to the business. If leaders nurture their team, prospective employees will hear about the organization's culture and how it values its

employees, making it more desirable when attracting new talent. This, in turn, will result in the organization's positive reputation growing in the marketplace.

2. Responding well to change. Businesses constantly change. If you embrace a more human approach, your team members will respond to change much better. They will ask questions, talk about the change, be open to new changes and challenges, and feel included in the change process.

3. Raising a future leader. When you show humanness in your approach and nurture the development of your staff, you are helping to raise the next generation of leaders. This means the business will be able to promote from within, and the organization will have fewer recruitment costs as employees will be happy and will want to stay!

There's no doubt that by showing compassion, being empathetic, and embracing our human side, we can lead in a way that helps others grow. This is a win-win situation! It benefits the employee who can develop, the leader who has a trustworthy and communicative team, and the business that grows and enjoys a more positive reputation as a result. All of that is because you are being YOU!

When you are a leader that others want to follow, you are a game-changer. However, that doesn't mean you are not vulnerable and will not make mistakes from time to time... because we are all still human! There's a lesson to be learned at every bump in the road. A competent leader owns this reality. They accept it, make it part of their learning journey, and use their mistakes to teach themselves and others.

In the next chapter, we'll focus on how you can provide effective feedback as a leader. Humanness is important here, too. Why? Because if you want your direct reports to really connect with you and take notice of your feedback, you can use what you've learned in this chapter to develop how you provide it.

9

THE 7 FEEDBACK STRATEGIES – WHAT'S THE BEST ONE FOR YOU?

eedback is an essential part of leadership. Once you find a winning strategy, you can start to use it to the advantage of your direct reports, the organization, and yourself. As a leader, you need to give direct, effective feedback. It must improve your employees' performance and encourage them to grow and develop.

The aim of feedback is to boost employees, not discourage them. There are 7 effective strategies you can use when giving feedback to individuals to ensure it's really impactful.

Why is feedback really important?

Leaders know that providing constructive feedback to their direct reports:

- Fuels motivation Improves performance
- Fosters growth Promotes loyalty
- Increases employee engagement Improves relationships and staff morale
- Provides a strategic way to give advice and guidance while aiming to develop employees

The impact of the feedback given depends on how it's *delivered*. This is the determining factor between success and failure. Many employees take feedback as only criticism. As a leader, it's up to you to frame the conversation properly to prevent this.

If feedback is negative or vague, it can demotivate employees. Even positive feedback can backfire and turn into negative feedback if employees feel it is hollow praise or insincere.

EFFECTIVE FEEDBACK STRATEGIES

Your most important task when delivering feedback is delivering it in a way that works for you and your direct reports. It's your job to get the most out of the conversation; this is why I recommended that you use the strategies below to deliver feedback in the most effective way.

1. **Purpose-driven**—You give employees feedback by hosting a mini-feedback session. You will focus on the end goal and discuss

how the employee can reach that goal. Your communication in the workplace will reflect this strategy.

2. **Tangible**—This is when you provide specific and tangible feedback, which again relates to an end goal. One of the most common complaints about feedback is that it is vague. So, if you want to provide tangible feedback, it must be direct and specific. Say, 'you did a good job with the report you prepared for me yesterday...' and then you can refer to something, in particular, you liked about it.

3. **Actionable** is when you provide feedback that focuses on things that can be acted upon immediately. A leader may find they have to change behaviors; in this case, they need to provide clear direction. If an employee is rude to other employees, you will have to identify how they are being rude, i.e., focus on the behavior (action), not the person— what did they do exactly? By pinpointing the specific behavior, they can more easily change it. Simply telling them, they were 'rude' to their colleague doesn't help them change.

4. **Focused**—A leader must be clear and direct. A common mistake managers make is to list all problems and file them away, then discuss them all at once. Problems and conflicts

should be addressed as they arise and directly. Saving them up is a mistake, as it will feel more like an attack on the person rather than feedback. They will feel undervalued as a result. Stay focused on the bigger picture instead and focus on one or two things at a time. Remember to assign timescales to check on results and objectives.

5. **Timely**—It's best to provide feedback at the moment, especially when you catch someone doing something *right*. If you acknowledge their success in public, it also reinforces that positive behavior in other team members. Positive feedback is a powerful motivator, but ensure you don't publicly discuss anything that is constructive. It's best to speak about that in private.

6. **Regular**—Feedback is something a leader should provide regularly. This isn't just a yearly event, saved for appraisals and annual performance reviews. To be impactful, it must be regular. It's best provided in a 1-on-1 conversation, at the moment, when needed, or when the occasion calls for it. Regular feedback conversations ensure that direct reports continuously perform to high standards. If a leader or manager regularly interacts with an employee, that employee is three times more likely to be engaged at work. This also helps build relationships

within the team and shows you are invested in your team.

7. **Consistent**—It's important that you are consistent when it comes to providing feedback. Workplaces bring enormous pressures at times, but as a leader, you must make time to interact with and provide feedback to your team consistently. It's your responsibility to carve out time in your day to ensure you are providing feedback. Have a feedback strategy and stick to it. Carve time out in your calendar. It's extremely important. Without it, your team will not perform to the best of their ability. They will lack direction and motivation.

Think of feedback as clearly identified road signs. Without them, everyone would be going around in circles!

Providing effective feedback to your team and direct reports is an effective way to manage your team and increase their morale and performance. You will notice a great difference if the feedback is constructive and consistent. This is because your workforce feels appreciated and valued. Positive relationships are formed as a result, and your direct reports will improve and grow. The whole organization will reap the benefits. Companies that provide consistent feedback enjoy an 8.9% increase in profitability, as reported by *Gallup*.

As an effective, early leader, consistent feedback is

not a luxury but a must. You also need to consider the authenticity you bring into your leadership role. This is the focus of the next chapter.

10

HOW TO BRING AUTHENTICITY INTO LEADERSHIP

*E*veryone wants a leader that they can trust, and it's up to you to build that trust between you and your direct reports. Authentic leader gets results, and—because they are genuine—they constantly develop their leadership style and lead with purpose.

> "*A genuine leader is not a searcher of consensus but a molder of consensus.*"
> ~ Martin Luther King. Jr.

When you're an authentic leader, people will respond. Let's face it that is what we all want to see! Breaking the mold and becoming one of the new generations of leaders means you really understand what it takes to lead people.

In this chapter, we'll explore how you can bring authenticity into leadership and the benefits that come with it. To know the 'how' and the 'why,' we must first consider what it means to be an authentic leader.

WHAT DOES IT MEAN TO BE AN AUTHENTIC LEADER?

Sometimes, people go into leadership roles and try to be something they're not. People will sense if you try to be someone other than yourself. Sooner or later, your true self will shine through. Hey, your true self might be just what the doctor ordered... but if you never show it, you will never know. People will question your authenticity, which will result in them mistrusting you.

Authenticity means you are true to yourself, first and foremost, regardless of the situations and barriers you face. When you become a leader, showing who you truly are become imperative. Difficult situations and idealized views formed by others often make it difficult for leaders to earn genuine respect or live up to their expectations. Carving out your path is both exciting and nerve-racking. Whatever you decide, decide fast. That way, you can make mistakes and improve your leadership style quickly.

Being authentic isn't always easy, as difficult situations in the early stages of leadership can test and challenge us.

Being authentic means, you are:

- Honest

- Genuine
- True to yourself

If you try to be anything other than that, you are not being authentic. Don't do it! Authenticity is important, especially in leadership roles, so let's address some of the benefits. These are not just for you but for your team as well.

THE BENEFITS: WHY DO WE NEED AN AUTHENTIC LEADER?

To be fully trusted by others, we need to be authentic. This plays a big role in increasing your credibility and visibility. Leaders who are seen to act in authentic ways are often said to be compelling and charismatic. In this way, an authentic leader organically commands respect and fosters goodwill.

Honesty is the best policy in business and in life! As a leader, you are a mentor to others. People look up to you. You must model authenticity for others to follow, respect, and trust you. They will then begin to mirror your behavior and act in a similar way. Authenticity breeds authenticity!

Authentic leadership allows you to gain a good reputation and reflects well on the organization.

HOW TO DEVELOP YOUR AUTHENTIC LEADERSHIP STYLE

There are a few steps to take if it's important for you to bring authenticity into your leadership. Great leaders understand the importance of building authentic relationships with their direct reports. They do this by:

1. **Becoming more self-aware is essential for every leader, as you must get to know your strengths and gaps, as well as what motivates you and your values.** The process of self-discovery can start with your own story, but it should move on to the things you've learned. It requires listening to feedback, digging deep into your strengths, developing emotional intelligence, and exploring your weaknesses or gaps.

2. **Understanding your personal values—** reflecting on your personal life will help you better understand your principles, values, and passions. You can then learn to apply your passions, influencing your lead. Having strong values is the foundation that fuels your fire and enables you to become a more confident, effective leader.

3. **Balancing your motivations—**when you start to explore your values and increase your self-awareness, you will gain insight into what motivates you. There are two types of motivations: *Extrinsic and intrinsic.* Extrinsic motivation is a common response when

measuring your success. It is all about tangible things, such as your car, home, money, etc. They are great short-term motivators. However, material things do not continuously sustain motivation. Leaders often begin to feel a lack of fulfillment due to a lack of meaning, as extrinsic motivators do not keep us motivated in the long term. Intrinsic motivations are more meaningful. They are closely linked to your values, which means they provide you with a sense of fulfillment that is lacking in extrinsic motivators. It's important that you strike the right balance between the two. Ensure you stay motivated by tangible things and fulfilled by intrinsic things.

4. **Finding and developing your support team** — leaders cannot succeed on their own; they need support and advice from others. These folks are often called 'sponsors' because their role is to be the person that has your back and will sponsor your ideas for improvement or change. In turn, authentic leaders build teams who support each other and stay focused. A team like this performs better as they provide each other with feedback, and a wide range of balanced perspectives and, as a result, are more fully engaged. The leader coaches and challenges their team in an authentic way.

5. **Personal and work-life balance**—a leader is balanced and consistent in all areas of their life when they are truly being authentic. They are good at balancing their personal life and their effective leadership abilities, and both realities often intertwine on the journey to authenticity. Allow this to happen, and all the while remaining professional. Once you've built strong work relationships with your team members, you will notice when they are being affected by burnout. Balancing the demands of work and personal life is difficult at the best of times, but it has now become much more difficult since most folks are working from home. We will talk about this further in chapter 28.

6. **Remember Your Roots**—If leaders are authentic, they need to stay grounded in their life. It's important to spend time with family and friends, exercise, enjoy your hobbies, and stay accountable. Spiritual practices can also help with this; they will remind you of your values and where you came from and allow you to drive toward your goals and passions. This is really useful if you want your authenticity to be sustainable. So, make it count, and make it last!

7. **Inspire and Empower Those Around You**— once you have raised your self-awareness, you can use your authentic voice to inspire

and empower others. Authentic leaders create a culture of loyalty and trust, and they're not afraid to be vulnerable and show their emotions… we are all only human! Through this, you will inspire your direct reports to lead or take on new roles and challenges. As a result, the organization will retain and develop its top talent while attracting other high-quality people with the same visions, values, and goals. It's a fact that authentic leaders produce sustainable results, which help the organization grow.

While developing your authentic leadership style requires courage and honesty, reflecting on your own experiences, understanding your values and motivators, and owning your story can help you strengthen yourself in your leadership role. It allows you to build trust and empower others. Learning to be authentic and embracing your leadership style brings you balance. It's an impactful, essential journey that must be made to reinforce your position as an effective leader!

11

UNLOCK EMPLOYEE ACTIVATION THROUGH PSYCHOLOGICAL SAFETY

*Y*ou have a responsibility to develop your direct reports. This has many benefits to you, the business, and to the employees themselves. But it isn't always easy. One way to do this is to unlock employee activation. Let's explore what that means.

Employee activation allows employees to organically and authentically create and share content about the topics that interest them. This is important, as it ensures that your employees are fully engaged, constructive, and trustworthy. Basically, you're helping them become authentic and optimally productive. An effective way to unlock employee activation is through what is called 'psychological safety.' Psychological safety happens when employees can speak up and express their ideas, concerns, and mistakes without fear of reprisal. Your direct reports will only do this if you create an environment that embodies safety.

Employee activation is one of the most impactful ways to build positive customer relationships and establish your brand as a thought leader. So, we will consider exactly what employee activation is, how you can promote it through psychological safety, and how it can benefit you as a leader and the business.

As a leader, you must lead your team well and encourage them to work in a way that's best for the business. This is impactful, as they will feel encouraged to build trust and strong connections with customers. In this chapter, we'll focus on how you can use the concept of psychological safety to spark your employees and get them working in ways that benefit everyone.

Let's explore some of those benefits...

THE BENEFITS OF EMPLOYEE ACTIVATION

Employee activation is the most impactful way to build positive relationships with customers and establish your brand as a thought leader. This popular marketing trend boosts business marketing efforts and engages customers.

Increases innovation—innovation is most likely to occur when employees feel able to speak up, take intelligent risks, and think creatively.

Higher employee retention—if you contribute to your employees' happiness, they will likely stay with the company longer. Creating an environment where they feel able to speak up, be valued, and be challenged, means you are more likely to retain them. This is easier for you, too, as you can build a team you can trust and get to know. For the business it's much more cost-effective for the business as recruitment can be costly and lengthy.

Better performance and productivity—it's a known fact that a happier workforce performs better and is more productive. Productivity is said to increase by up to 25% due to employee activation.

Improved reputation—high-performing and happy teams contribute to the business and allow for its reputation to flourish, especially if that business promotes from within. We all want to be a part of an organization we feel we have a future and can contribute to our success.

A good reputation boosts employee retention by 18%

We've talked about the benefits of employee activation, but let's get super clear about what employee activation means.

WHAT IS EMPLOYEE ACTIVATION?

As mentioned earlier, employee activation can be a program—or simply an opportunity—for employees to freely share information and their leader, allowing them to grow and develop their knowledge and skills. In essence, it sparks the mind of the employee.

Consider the term 'activate.' It means that something has become operative or active. You are essentially flipping the mind on like a switch as a leader.

Employee activation encourages employees to engage, create, and share content about topics that interest them and enhance their development. Many organizations use this as a marketing tool. The idea is that the topics they are interested in relate to their work and can help the business strengthen its brand while exciting your ideal clients about being in business with your organization.

This concept delves so much deeper than marketing because, in many cases, it boosts morale and translates to higher returns on investment.

There are many ways to activate your direct reports. You can offer robust training and work shadowing and challenge them by offering an opportunity to participate in project work or problem-solving within the business. This chapter will focus on how you can activate your direct reports through psychological safety.

USING PSYCHOLOGICAL SAFETY TO ACTIVATE EMPLOYEES

Psychological safety occurs when your direct reports believe they can share their opinions, questions, ideas, mistakes, and concerns without embarrassment, punishment, or humiliation. In order to do this right, your team members need to feel that their workplace is safe. You can facilitate this by ensuring that the company atmosphere within the team is open, accepting, and honest.

Only 30% of employees feel that their opinions are considered at work. This can cause problems as your direct reports may feel undervalued or not listened to, which further lowers morale and productivity in the workplace. This can also negatively impact your employees—if they feel stressed, they may not speak up.

It's your job to ensure you adopt a psychologically safe environment for your team and all teams. In return, employees will work effectively and feel able to express their options. Safe environments also promote other characteristics that create an effective team, such as increasing dependability and reliability, providing structure and clarity within the team, and giving the team a purpose and meaning. In turn, this enhances the team's impact as each member knows that their work counts.

On an individual level, psychological safety activates your direct reports as it promotes a high-performing work culture, fosters engagement, and initiates a higher level of collaboration. It also encourages employees to explore new forms of creativity organically and develops their thinking skills.

TWO MAIN INGREDIENTS FOR PSYCHOLOGICAL SAFETY

There are two main ingredients involved in fostering a psychologically safe workplace. These are:

1. **Listening**—you must listen to what employees have to say and allow time and space for sharing ideas and opinions. Everyone needs to have the opportunity to take part, and it's important that employees are aware that their time and input count. No idea is a silly idea. You could even have a suggestion box or online shared forum for staff to post their ideas and feedback.

2. **Empathy**—it's a good idea to put yourself in your employee's shoes and foster an open environment, encouraging staff to be open-minded and supportive of each other. Empathy is a key driver of psychological safety, so don't simply nod your head; really listen and consciously consider their point of view. You can summarize the conversation in your own words, ask questions, and take notes. This shows that you recognize and value their input.

If your goal is to create a psychologically safe environment, then actively listening and showing empathy is the name of the game! This is truly leading by example. In earlier chapters, we talked about diversity; it's important to remember that this also helps foster psychological safety, ensuring that nobody feels excluded.

By embracing psychological safety, you will ignite a team of engaged high performers who understand their value. They will easily express their unique viewpoints and expertise, and you will begin to notice a culture shift within the organization as your team becomes 'activated.' This means that employees will become more engaged and inspired, and your team members will grow and develop their skills much more quickly and easily. When your employees are activated, they will be able to engage and inspire your clients as well. If this is the type of team you want, you have no choice but to create a psychologically safe environment.

They deserve it! You deserve it! The business deserves it! That's what we call a Win-Win!

FOSTERING UPWARD COMMUNICATION

*U*pward communication is becoming increasingly popular, as other, more traditional methods are becoming less so. While you likely do not need to be told how important communication is in business, it is worth mentioning that communication within the business— especially upward communication—is key.

Upward communication can be intimidating because it challenges an organization's culture and changes how employees perceive authority figures. Leaders who are open to this type of communication are more likely to know what is happening in the business because communication channels are open.

In this chapter, we'll focus on the importance of upward communication, its challenges, and how we can encourage it in the workplace. Once you foster this approach as a leader, you'll find that your direct reports find it easier to share their ideas, provide feedback, and raise concerns in their day-to-day.

WHAT IS UPWARD COMMUNICATION, AND WHY IS IT IMPORTANT FOR ME?

Upward communication is how employees directly communicate with those in a more senior role. For example, it's how your team members communicate with you, other leaders, managers, and senior leadership. Traditionally, communication was downward. Managers would communicate with those they were senior to. But upward communication is becoming more and more important in forward-thinking businesses.

Upward communication encourages others to share their ideas, provide feedback, and raise any relevant concerns. It's a way for businesses to find out what's happening within the organization. It encourages inclusivity, participation, and engagement. SIS International Research suggests that businesses lose more than $525,000 annually due to ineffective communication between managers and employees. So, communication is proving more important than ever.

Organizations that foster upward communication benefit because it provides workplace transparency makes decision-making easier gives employees a better experience at work, and ensures better team collaboration. When employees feel they can speak up, they are much more likely to trust the organization and its people. Improved communication creates a healthier work environment, which improves engagement and staff retention, as staff feels valued and included. Managers and leaders who accept feedback from their employees find that relationships flourish, especially if the leader responds appropriately or takes positive action in response.

Communication helps employees and leaders align regarding the company's vision, mission, and goals. Strong communication channels enable everyone to engage and strive towards a unified target or goal. Employees will be willing to share their knowledge and collaborate if they feel valued and included, as they will also foster this approach. You'll find that they share skills and knowledge and help each other develop more freely and frequently. Contributing their knowledge and experiences in this way has a positive effect on broader organizational performance.

Undoubtedly, upward communication leads to innovation because employees aim for their full potential. As a leader, you must recognize the importance of giving your employees a voice! Of course, upward communication doesn't come without its challenges... so let's look at some of those.

THE CHALLENGES OF UPWARD COMMU-NICATION

The main challenge of upward communication is getting everybody on board and moving against traditional methods. Making the transition is typically not very smooth, as there are several problems that you may encounter:

1. **Unwillingness**—sometimes, your direct reports may feel unwilling to start this as it doesn't come easily to them. Speaking up is sometimes seen as challenging authority, and employees may not want to do this in the beginning as it feels unnatural. You need to set their minds at ease.
2. **Fear**—employees often fear that they could be negatively affected if they let their superiors know about their challenges. This will become easier as the practice becomes more established, but it may take you some time to build trust first.
3. **By-passing**—due to the nature of upward communication, your direct reports could decide to make a suggestion or share ideas with your manager. That can be difficult for the person who has been bypassed, which could cause confrontation. Make sure you are fully prepared for this to happen, and don't take it personally. Discuss it with your direct report afterward and find out how it can be avoided next time. Once you understand their reasons, you might be able to prevent it from happening again in the future.

4. **Overuse**—occasionally, your employees may use the idea of upward communication to contact leaders and managers too much. They may behave in a desperate way that disrupts the chain of command. While upward communication is innovative, a balance must be maintained, and employees must consider when it's appropriate and when it is not.

5. **Making mistakes**—sometimes, employees are unaware of all aspects of the business, so they may make mistakes when communicating information or data, as there are things they may not have considered. This can be embarrassing and may knock their confidence regarding upward communication. You can encourage them to seek advice if they are unsure!

While upward communication brings some challenges that you must face head-on as a leader, it's still worthwhile to foster this method of communication. Let's move on and talk about how you can begin to encourage communication in the workplace the right way.

HOW TO ENCOURAGE UPWARD COMMUNICATION IN THE WORKPLACE

It's your role to encourage upward communication

and drive it forward. There are a few ways you can encourage it by...

The most important thing is getting other leaders and managers onboard, as their cooperation is crucial, and the approach must be consistent. It can be difficult for managers to encourage their employees to raise their voices. While you cannot force this, you can build a culture of open communication—which includes managers and leaders—that promotes interaction between all staff through open lines of communication. In this way, like group forums and digital open-door policies, employees can communicate without fear.

To make the transition to upward communication, it's a good idea to understand the employees and their state of mind. Remember, they may find this uncomfortable initially, but you need to keep working on communication and encourage them to adapt their efforts. Ensure it's relevant but appropriately personal. For example, refer to them by name, and—if you know a little about what they've been working on—ask them how it's going. Showing interest in them can make communication easier, but ensure you choose the right type of communication. *Will an email or meeting suffice, or is a 1-on-1 chat better?*

Employees may avoid communication when in groups, so ensure you create opportunities for everyone to express their concerns, feedback, or ideas. Open channels for them to ask questions or comment on your announcements. If you urge your direct reports to create and share their content, it will encourage more communication as the employees will then be organically driving the narrative. You can then lead the conversation and give it purpose!

Another way to encourage upward communication is by being authentic and approachable. You're familiar with authenticity already, but if you are friendly and have created a culture of open communication, your employees will find it far easier to approach you. Showing the real, you will help to relieve any unease and anxiety they may feel about upward communication. You will need to remain authentic and keep your employees up to date with as much inspiring internal content as possible. This will keep them engaged and get on board with adopting upward communication.

Keeping track of how it's going can help you discover what works and what doesn't when motivating your team. Measuring this will help you review the difference upward communication makes to the team and the organization. If you understand what is driving your employees, you can use this data to make and drive future decisions.

Communication is important in business, especially when you need to pass on information or request it. As important as communication is in the workplace, delegation is just as important. In the next chapter, we'll discuss ways you can become more comfortable with delegation.

13

DELEGATE LIKE A PRO

Being able to delegate is a key skill required of all leaders and managers. As a leader, you must be able to assign tasks appropriately. Being able to do this will enhance your performance and the performance of your team.

Delegation isn't simply about telling others what to do or how to do something. It's a strategic act that takes contemplation but also sometimes requires quick thinking. In this chapter, we'll consider why this is so important, how we can overcome the barriers we face as leaders when we assign tasks to others, and how can we delegate effectively. Being able to delegate work shows our awareness of our direct reports and their skills. By the end of this chapter, you'll feel able to do this with confidence and feel assured in your choices when it comes to delegation.

We'll start by exploring the reasons why this is so important!

WHY DO WE NEED TO DELEGATE?

Delegation is a key business skill that all leaders and managers should master. It's a leadership quality that shows you know your team members and their capabilities. A Gallup study recently found that companies led by CEOs who are confident and efficient delegators perform better and achieve a higher growth rate. You're probably wondering why this is, but it can be summed up in a single statement...

Delegation gets things done!!!

We've already talked about getting to know your direct reports and what they are good at. Using this knowledge to assign work to the most appropriate employee ensures that the right person completes the right job. That person is the most likely to succeed, and therefore you are guaranteeing that the project will get done properly and on time. This has numerous benefits for both the individual and the whole team:

The projects are completed on time and within budget. Your team member feels empowered as you've set them up to win.

Other team members will learn from that employee's autonomy and strengths, which will encourage them to think in a more creative way and approach things differently. It will also encourage them to want to be involved.

You are demonstrating trust by giving ownership of an important task to a specific team member. Your team will then recognize that they are an important part of the whole.

It improves efficiency, as no leader can do all things at all times—this boosts team morale and improves performance.

There are also benefits of delegation for you. It allows you to free up some of your time to deal with more pressing matters. It also encourages you to prioritize your tasks, and—while you'll still be overseeing the task—it also empowers your team and supports them in developing new skills. You'll find that trust develops as you trust your employees. It is, therefore, mutually beneficial and strengthens relationships.

OVERCOMING THE BARRIERS

There are some barriers that you may face as an early leader who delegates, especially if this is something you have not done before and it's not a skill that comes naturally to you. It takes patience and practice, but it's nothing that you can't handle. In fact, you've worked on some key leadership skills already that will help you conquer the challenges you may be facing in your role. A leader can face two main barriers when they delegate: reluctance and uncertainty (not knowing who to delegate to). Let's explore this further.

Sometimes when you instruct another team member to do something, you may face reluctance. They may not know how to perform a specific task, or you haven't built enough trust yet. Being an authority figure who is respected by their team is important, so ensure that the foundation is strong. Be confident that the person who is doing the task can do it, is supported, and wants the team to succeed. Make sure that the person you trust with a task is someone you have already started building trust with. Set clear objectives and check in regularly to ensure they stay on track.

Another common barrier to effective delegation is considering which of your direct reports has the right skills to complete the task in question. When assigning tasks, you need to set your team members up to succeed, not fail. This becomes much easier when you get to know your team and learn about their strengths. Sometimes, this takes a little time to perfect, but you can do it. Start with smaller, easier tasks of lower importance and increase their difficulty or level of importance. This way, you can build your confidence when it comes to assigning tasks to your team members, and it will also encourage your direct reports' development.

HOW TO DELEGATE EFFECTIVELY

Effective delegation is one of the most difficult transitions that a leader must make, as they have to shift from their 'individual contributor' role to allowing and trusting others to complete tasks competently and independently. When a leader is new, many colleagues, peers, and higher-level managers admire their ability to roll up their sleeves and get the job done, but you can only do that for so long. While you may want to hold onto the most tactical assignments at first, you have to learn to let go and trust in your team. This is tough—even for the seasoned leader—so don't feel bad if you find this challenging at first. The key is to practice and maintain an open dialogue with your team about their progress.

For most leaders and managers, responsibilities become much more complex. Our human tendencies, such as not wanting to hurt or offend anyone make our job more difficult... yet we must remain efficient. Effective delegation ensures this happens. Otherwise, you're in danger of becoming a super-sized contributor and not the leader you need to be. By working on engaging your team and encouraging them to contribute, their actions can extend your presence. This will raise the bar when it comes to your leadership potential. You'll often find that they enjoy contributing to the shared priorities and will produce their best work as a result. Remember, this is a good thing! It's up to you to raise more effective leaders.

If you really want to set the table for effective delegation, be clear and firm. You will shape how your direct reports perceive the tasks you give them while encouraging them to take ownership of that work.

There are five principles you can follow to ensure you delegate effectively:

- Express why something is important to you
- Clarify your expectations—have they been clearly communicated?
- Ask how much you need to be involved—are they willing to take the reins?
- Practice saying 'no.'
- Ask them to set goals and deadlines (obviously, with your input).

It's important that you don't focus on execution, so hold back from considering the bigger picture of leading and stay focused on the now. If you show confidence when delegating by following these principles, the work will get done because the right people will be focused on the right tasks.

Delegating effectively not only builds trust but it also empowers your team and encourages professional development. You also learn more about your direct reports in the process and can start to figure out who is best suited to tackling specific projects or tasks. Assigning tasks and instructing others are key components of a leader's role—you can't and shouldn't do everything yourself. In the next chapter, we'll discuss motivating employees further through spotlighting and recognition. As a powerful leader who has the capacity to inspire others to lead, you're certainly up for *this* challenge!

14

SPOTLIGHT AND RECOGNIZE EFFECTIVELY

*W*e can sometimes become consumed by our work.

This means we don't always make time to recognize the work our team delivers. Your staff deserves recognition for their contributions and dedication as they ensure the business's success. From time to time, they need to feel appreciated and recognized. As a leader, you can use recognition to help motivate your employees. This has never been more important than now, during the 'great resignation.'

Spotlighting is an important motivator, and it's an excellent tool that can be used to show your appreciation in a public setting.

In this chapter, we'll focus on how you can spotlight effectively and explore different types of recognition, the benefits of recognition, and other possible reward ideas. Recognizing your team members is a positive affirmation that helps them alter their subconscious beliefs and encourages them to adopt a more positive outlook. This positively impacts the business, as being optimistic increases productivity and performance.

Let's give our employees the recognition they deserve!

TYPES OF EMPLOYEE RECOGNITION

The trouble with recognition is that every employee embraces it differently. While some prefer subtle praise, others like it to be public. It's important that every leader considers this when showing appreciation. Let's look at some of the different ways you can praise others:

1. **Private or Social**—some people prefer subtle praise when they're alone, while others prefer to be praised in front of others. You should tailor your recognition style to meet your direct reports' needs.
2. **Anonymous or Attributed**—anonymous recognition is subtle, and many people prefer this style; however, generally, it is provided so that they know where it's coming from. Placing a thank, you note on someone's desk, a comment in the company newsletter, or giving someone an anonymous shout-out is a powerful way to commend your direct reports. While some people will appreciate

such anonymous gestures, others will prefer to know who is giving them the recognition.

3. **Superior or Peer**—while it's good to be recognized by superior staff members, most people also appreciate it when it comes from their colleagues/fellow team members. Recognition from all levels feels good, and a leader can encourage their team to recognize and praise each other as well.

4. **Achievement or Behavior**—leaders often praise others based on specific achievements or metrics, but it's good to recognize general positive behavior in others. For example, if a colleague works extra hours to meet a deadline or if they go the extra mile for a customer or coworker.

You must discover how your colleagues/employees prefer to receive their recognition. By being aware of the different types, you can adapt your style to meet the preferences of your direct reports. This will ensure they take pride in their work and remain motivated. Spotlighting is a great way to encourage your direct reports to shine and succeed. Whatever you decide to do, remember to do it authentically. Your recognition needs to be meaningful to the person being recognized. It's a good practice to let them know what they are being recognized for and why. Inauthentic recognition generally doesn't land well.

SPOTLIGHTING AND ITS BENEFITS

A spotlight highlights achievements, accomplishments, successes, personality, background, and anniversaries that are important to employees and their success. By placing them in the limelight, you show your recognition publicly by telling the world about your top employees and how they've contributed to the business.

A leader who spotlights their employees shows how much they appreciate them and their pivotal role in the business's success. The benefits of spotlighting include the following:

1. **Boosting recruitment strategies**—employee spotlights help businesses to attract the very best. That means you have a high-quality workforce, and your employees are further motivated to shine. **Ensuring connections with employees are meaningful**—you get to know them better when you get the opportunity to interview and write about your direct reports. You're, therefore, more likely to communicate more effectively and break down any communication barriers. This allows leaders to make more meaningful connections with their employees.

2. **Increasing social media engagement and reach**—you'll find that employee spotlights are popular on social media, and others are

more likely to share them. The employee may share the good news with their families and friends. Content like this gets picked up a lot more than sales messages do and makes a positive statement about the company as it appears to be firmly invested in its people.

3. **Winning potential client contracts—** employee spotlights allow the business to create a human face for itself. Therefore, if you are bidding for contracts or working with another business, the client's decision may be based on whom they think is the best fit. *Would you prefer to work with a company that appreciates every employee or an organization without a strong culture?*

4. **Improving the business's reputation—**an employee spotlight shows that you invest time and money in your employees. This demonstrates that your company cares for its people. Other customers and businesses will notice this, and it will improve your public image, which can help to attract both prospective employees and clients.

5. **Improving existing relationships with clients—** your spotlights aren't simply used for winning new contracts or customers; they can also help improve existing relationships. Existing clients can reaffirm their commitment to working with you, and they could even take up the opportunity to engage

with your brand or your staff in a closer capacity.

CREATING EMPLOYEE SPOTLIGHT

Many leaders are unsure of how to create an employee spotlight. In truth, it is a simple process. You must ask yourself three key questions:

Who to highlight? It's possible for anyone in your business to be spotlighted, so ensure you are inclusive unless they have expressed that they do not want to be included! If an employee does want to participate, ensure you highlight a wide cross-section of your team. You must remember that everyone deserves to be recognized! So, find other ways to recognize it in private.

What to include in your spotlight? Many elements of an employee spotlight must be included—a picture of your employee, their name/job title, and a direct quote. Consider adding more detail. This will help your reader engage in the spotlight, as they likely want to know more. For example, you could include a detailed description of their role and indicate how long they've worked for the organization. You then need to consider some questions and answers related to their job (before you cover things like their hobbies outside of work). It's up to you as a leader to help your employees shine, so feel free to ask other questions. Try to find out some interesting facts. You could ask your employees about the company culture, why they like their job and/or their role, and any company perks they enjoy. You can do this as a written question-and-answer session, video, or voice-recorded interview. They need to let the outside world know, in an authentic way, how it feels to work for your organization. Don't focus too much on the questions and answers. Keep it short, sweet, and fresh. Don't be afraid to talk more about anything interesting your employee shares.

Where to show your spotlight?

EVERYWHERE!

Don't be afraid to post your employee spotlights all over the place—from your websites to Facebook pages or groups, or even post them on your company blog! Facebook, Twitter, and LinkedIn are great platforms to use if you want to get your spotlights out to an engaged audience.

You could even use snippets for advertising the whole spotlight interview. Videos could be uploaded to your company's YouTube account and then shared from there.

It's a fact employee spotlights transform businesses, so this is something you can certainly take the time to do. The benefits for the employee, your company, and you as a leader are endless.

OTHER EMPLOYEE REWARD IDEAS

There are other ways to motivate your employees, such as by providing them with rewards. One way is to get your team members together and have them nominate the person they felt kicked butt with last week and why. You can then commend achievements together and celebrate with the most nominations.

Some businesses name people on their staff website as a feature and congratulate employees who have performed extremely well—for example, Employee of the Month. This can be similar to a spotlight, as the post will recognize employees in other aspects of their life and work. A team message book works well too, where people can leave each other messages that share wins or congratulations for either a personal or professional event. These can then be read out at your weekly team meeting— you could even include personal wellness or health as a category as well!

There are many forms that recognition can take, but the most effective are public. Everyone celebrating wins together increases team spirit! As a leader, you must ensure that incentives or rewards align with the company's core values and message.

Now we've discussed how you can lead your direct reports, we're about to move on to Section III and talk about leading your team as a whole unit. It's time to be the people leader your team deserves!

SECTION III - LEADING A TEAM

There's no doubt about it—teams reflect their managers and leaders. So, if you are an effective, proactive manager then you increase the chances of success for your team. It's not always easy leading a diverse team, especially in the beginning. You're likely still developing your own skills, while simultaneously being expected to inspire and develop each one of your employees... that's a big responsibility! But it's certainly one you can rise to.

"Leadership is about making others better as a result of your presence and making sure that impact lasts in your absence."
~ Sheryl Sandberg

When you are a new leader managing a team, you must learn to get to know and manage your direct reports individually. It's also important you learn to lead them all together, as one unit. This brings your team closer, and as a result, they will work more efficiently towards common goals by helping and supporting one another more consistently. This section focuses on how you can create your team vision and how you can bring it to life. It involves getting to know your team and how they work while exploring their strengths and gaps. We'll also explore syncing goals, the importance of trust within the team, and the ways that you can coach your team to greatness. We have lots to do so let's get started.

15

THE SHARED VISION - HOW TO BRING IT TO LIFE

*E*veryone has a vision. A business has a vision, its managers and leaders have a vision, and the employees within the business do as well. The issue? They aren't always aligned.

This chapter explores how to create a clear vision and how it can be used to inspire others so that they can share in that dream. They can then align themselves, resulting in everyone working towards the same goals and having similar expectations.

Your vision is your ideal. It's the visual objective you are aiming for in the future. You need to figure out how you're going to get there now. Imagine you want to climb Mount Everest one year from now. First, you would need to work out how to train and prepare for such an event. Once you have a training plan, you then need to fit that plan into your existing schedule and ensure you make the deadline.

Leading a team isn't so different—you need an effective action plan.

But how do we ensure our new projects align with our vision, and how can we use this to inspire our team?

Let's look at this in more detail...

HOW CAN WE ENSURE EVERYTHING ALIGNS?

Having a clear vision will inspire your team. It can give them the sense of direction they need to succeed and achieve their goals. Your vision is the foundation of your goal-setting and action planning. For that reason, it must be strong. When you're taking on a new project, there are three questions you need to consider:

1. How can I align my daily goals, tasks, and vision?
2. When things are tough, what will keep me motivated?
3. Who will provide me with support?

The most innovative leaders can create an inspirational description of where they want to take their organization so that others will follow and support their efforts. That is their vision, and alignment results from others getting on board with it. *But it isn't always easy...*

Your dream must align with the business and its employees. It needs to be viable and what is best for all involved; otherwise, you risk spending your valuable time persuading people to buy into your idea! In most cases, people become compliant with—rather than committed to—the cause. A shared vision energizes the team, which encourages commitment and motivation. The key is to ensure that your foresight becomes the team's vision, and you can create this by increasing their level of involvement in its development.

The more in-depth your plan is, the more likely it is that your team will buy into it. You need to find ways of getting team members to believe in your vision... because if everyone isn't invested, you'll be fighting a losing battle! Your vision will only become a reality if others are open to making it theirs as well!

11 STEPS TO FOLLOW IF YOU WANT YOUR TEAM MEMBERS TO BE ALIGNED WITH YOUR VISION

Getting others to align with your dreams means investing time, which takes a great deal of commitment. There are 11 steps you can follow if alignment is your end goal:

1. **Decide who will be involved**—this is most likely to be your team members, but in some cases, you may choose to ask other teams or stakeholders to be involved (if they are an asset to your vision).
2. **Book time to collaborate**—schedule enough time to get everyone working towards the shared vision together. Make sure you work

somewhere you won't be disturbed. Try and book out a full day, and minimize interruptions, to stimulate creativity and construct a well-thought-out plan of action. However, if you are doing this virtually or already in a hybrid model, schedule smaller, bite-size meetings. I don't recommend anything over sixty minutes, as virtual fatigue is real! Chances are that people will struggle to maintain focus for more than sixty minutes.

3. **Assign someone to facilitate who is neutral** — this means you can take part in the meeting and focus on the task at hand rather than having to worry about facilitating and note-taking simultaneously. Your commitment to the conversation will increase the involvement of the rest of the team.

4. **Prepare in advance**—make sure that the collaboration day is booked well in advance, as this will ensure you can prepare. Ensure you send out documents and any other relevant information ahead of time, including any survey results, market research, or details of your competitors. Set and communicate pre-work expectations so your team feels involved before the collaboration occurs. This will allow you to follow up before the event so

that you can address any questions. It will also allow for the less outspoken team members to prepare their contributions. If you ask for their feedback, let them know ahead of time.

5. **Set the scene**—at the beginning of the meeting, review the desired outcomes of the collaboration, run through the agenda, set ground rules, and talk through the process. You can also check on the pre-work and everyone's thoughts. This sets the scene for the rest of the meeting and ensures everyone will know what to expect.

6. **Create your action plan**—if you want your team's full engagement and participation, you must encourage openness, creativity, and efficiency throughout the meeting. Your agenda will help you map out the collaboration day and help you put together your plan. If you have someone else who is facilitating, they can help with this. Your plan of action needs to detail your end goal and the steps and processes you will use to reach it.

7. **Don't worry about composing your shared vision statement just yet**—time with your team should not be wasted by perfectly crafting an elegant vision statement. Do this after the event if you can, or ask a couple of team members to take the lead. You can

communicate by email at a later date to figure it out.

8. **Speak in private with those who disagree—** we don't always agree on everything, so if a team member is not aligned, have a chat with them in private. See if they remain committed to the vision and explore different ways to help them re-engage. Link the vision to their needs, ideas, and interests.

9. **After the meeting—**you will need to come together after the vision statement has been drafted and discuss it. Ask everyone to contribute and make changes to perfect it.

10. **Catch up with other relevant parties who are not present at the meeting—**it's up to you to review the draft with other people who require involvement. This could be managers, peers, suppliers, customers, and other stakeholders. You can use their input to make further improvements.

11. **Once it is ready, it's time to make your vision a reality by communicating it to the world!** Partner with some of the company's most creative colleagues and ask them to help spread the word and bring it to life. Remember... you want to inspire! So, use images, stories, and metaphors to get the point across.

Involving others in your shared vision encourages

them to take ownership and commit to this idea. They will feel invested in the vision and will be more likely to align with it. The more people who believe in it, the higher the chances you will achieve it.

As an inspirational leader, make it your mission to get as many people as possible—to strive for—a shared vision that you all believe in!

You will easily recognize their strengths and values if you already know your team well and work well together. You can use this knowledge to get them invested in your vision from the start. Doing this at the beginning of a new year has been proven to have amazing results, but it can be done anytime you get a new team or become promoted to a new leadership role. The idea is to make it happen. Align on the shared vision and work towards it year-round.

Next, we'll focus on another important topic when it comes to leading a team—and that is, *knowing who they are.*

16

HOW WELL DO YOU KNOW YOUR TEAM?

*a*sk yourself, *HOW WELL DO YOU REALLY KNOW YOUR TEAM?*

A leader who knows their team gets the best from their team... period! But getting to *really* know them isn't that simple, as we can't just force people to open up to us. We have to work on this over time, but there are some things you can do to speed up the process.

This chapter focuses on the different strategies to use if you want to get to know your employees better. We'll explore how you can move beyond 'small talk' and into much deeper, more revealing conversations. We'll also discover how to make meetings more interesting, for team-building purposes.

> *"The strength of the team is each member. The strength of each member is the team."*
> ~ Phil Jackson

Raising an effective team is your job as a manager but getting to know them can be a complex task. Finding out the strengths of your team members improves the strength of the team as a whole, but everyone has a part to play. Let's explore how you can do your part by getting the ball rolling today!

BEYOND SMALL TALK

When you manage a new team, you have to understand every member. There are many reasons why this doesn't happen instantaneously, but there are several questions you can ask to gain more insight. If you want to get to know them, you could ask:

1. What are your favorite tasks to work on? *It's important to know this information as you'll often find that while some people love specific tasks, others strongly dislike them. Delegate these tasks accordingly, they will be more likely to enjoy their roles and will be more engaged!*
2. Can you tell me what you feel your strengths are? *Taking an interest in your team members and what they believe they are good at, excites them. They will appreciate your interest in them and will be more likely to open up.*
3. Is there anything your previous managers have done that you would or wouldn't like me to do? *This gives you credibility, as you are showing your team that you care. You will gain*

valuable insight into their preferences and what makes them tick. It will show them you aspire to be a better leader.

4. What are your career goals, and how are you working towards them? *Finding out the career goals of your team members means you can help them develop. After all, that's a key responsibility of a leader. This information will help you develop your relationship and advocate on their behalf, as you want to help them achieve their dreams. This builds morale and motivation as you are taking an interest in their learning and career progression.* Where did your previous manager or leader leave off with your career goals? *By asking this, you are indicating that you care and are willing to help develop their career.* When it comes to feedback, what works best for you... and how do you prefer to receive it (email, one-to-one, etc...)? *Asking this shows that you are interested in their well-being and how they feel. You need a person to be receptive to your feedback, so if it's delivered on their terms then they will be much more receptive to what you have to say.* What are your preferences when it comes to recognition and praise? How do you prefer to receive it? *Praise and recognition are tricky, because some people are comfortable with this publicly, while others prefer it to be more discreet. Find out what style your team members like so*

*you can ensure they feel comfortable receiving it.
Catering to their needs will build a stronger
bond.*

5. Tell me, what do you do outside of work?
*There's life beyond work, so make sure you take
an interest in the lives of your team members.
Start by considering their hobbies and things they
like to do before you move on to more personal
things like family or friends.*

6. What's really important to you? *Finding out
what's important to your team members will help
you find out what they really value in life. This
will give you insights into what they are really
like.*

Asking questions such as these will help you build a
strong rapport with each of your team members, but
you must develop the team rapport too. You need to
consider how to bring your team together. An effective
team is a whole-team effort, after all. So, let's talk
through some of the ways you can host meetings with a
difference...

HOSTING MEETINGS WITH A DIFFERENCE

There are ways you can get to know your team
members AND encourage teamwork. This is great for
you as a leader, as it will help you to get to know your
team and gauge how they can work best together.
Leaders are known for their innovation, so it's impor-

tant that you go beyond meetings and take things to the next level.

A leader must recognize that their employees are their greatest asset and know how they contribute to the business. Knowing this will allow you to harmonize how they work together as a team. This can be done by:

1. **Managing like a mentor**—if you manage like a mentor, you will form different relationships with your team. It will show them that you are interested in their career, and they will feel inspired by you and value your opinion as a result. The more you know about each of your team members, the easier it is to harmonize your team. **Team-building** —this is an excellent way to promote teamwork. You can play many different games, such as trivia, virtual board games, sport competitions, and brain-teasers, or you could simply use a deck of cards. It could be work-related or non-work-related, but it should be interesting and fun to help the team get to know each other.

2. **Hosting Town Hall sessions**—this is where a leader hosts sessions that communicate company plans, news, visions, goals, and strategies. This allows you to be transparent about the company and what its hopes are for the future, as well as its current position. It gives your team members the opportunity to

ask questions, which makes them feel valued by their organization.

3. **Attending lunch with your team members** — listening to them in this setting can help you establish a better relationship. You can work out what's on their mind, and being away from the office provides a more social, relaxed setting. This brings energy to the team and gives you insight into how your team members communicate with each other.

4. **Being yourself**—be vulnerable, authentic, and real when with your team. This will help build trust. If you want to be a great leader, you need to lead as your true self and avoid pretending to be anything you're not.

5. **Going to company social events and gatherings**—always make company events and gatherings a priority, as they are a great way to socialize with your team and take part in team-building activities. Communicating on a social level shows that you care about the well-being of your team.

6. **Getting your staff to reintroduce themselves at meetings**—formal introductions are always good, but there are so many things that you don't know! So, ask each team member to introduce themselves at each meeting and share a fun fact. This will allow other members of the team to get to know their colleagues on a more personal

level. **Working alongside your team**—you'll get to know your team better if you work alongside them. You'll be able to see how they work, including how they perform under pressure and communicate with their teammates. Lead by example, be as productive as possible and allow time for short breaks, refreshments, and chats. This will help you form a strong rapport and gauge how your team works together.

7. **Allowing dialogue**—if you want strong communication, you should encourage two-way dialogue in which your team members can communicate, and you can respond. This is effective, as employees will be able to share any worries, ideas, or suggestions. Communication is the key to success in business and life!

Getting to know your team ensures you can lead in a more innovative way. It improves communication, gives you direction as you'll get to know your staff better, and ensures you recognize what they are good at and how they can contribute to team and business goals. It's your opportunity to ensure everyone works together towards the same goal. This is an important step to take if you want to be able to confidently assign appropriate tasks and responsibilities to your team members and ensure your team performs and grows. We'll explore this further in the next chapter.

KNOW EVERY MEMBERS' STRENGTHS AND GROWTH AREAS

*I*n the previous chapter, we focused on how well you know your team. We mentioned knowing their strengths and growth areas. This is important for you to understand as a leader so that you can assign responsibilities and tasks to the right people.

In this chapter, we're going to delve deeper into this and focus on how you can find out more about the various strengths of your team members, so you can use these to the advantage of the business and your team. You can then develop plans to address their growth areas which will help your employees improve their skills and build experience along the way.

First off, let's look at why it's important for you to understand the strengths of your team members...

WHY DO I NEED TO UNDERSTAND THE STRENGTHS OF MY TEAM MEMBERS?

Understanding the strengths of your team members will help them feel more motivated and engaged when at work. It is also the steadiest way to help your company achieve its long-term or larger goals.

Understanding the assets of each of your team members is a practice in psychology. It helps you to align talent with relevant work opportunities, and it empowers your direct reports. But in order to get good at understanding them, you really have to know what they do well and what they need to improve on.

Let's look at the key ways you can begin to understand the strengths and growth areas of each person on your team.

13 WAYS TO FIND OUT YOUR TEAM MEMBER'S STRENGTHS

Before assigning tasks and responsibilities to the individuals on your team, you need to find out what they're good at. There are 13 easy ways to do this:

1. Ask great questions—questions provide you with the opportunity to find out more about your employees, and you'll learn how to leverage their strengths in the process. Be inquisitive by asking things like, *what tasks are you doing when you lose track of time?* Or, *what do you think your best attributes are?* Don't be afraid to also discuss strengths so you can match tasks to a team member's strengths.

2. Find out what tasks and responsibilities make them feel revitalized—doing tasks we are good at is great. But doing tasks we enjoy is a big motivator, so speak to your team and find out what energizes them. *What do they enjoy? What excites them?* If you leverage this, you'll see higher rates of productivity and progress. Don't discount anything they say, as they may have some unique talents you previously knew nothing about!

3. Use assessment testing, as this will help you to leverage the strengths of your team members— teams need to know how to leverage their unique strengths and talents. Using strength-finder assessments, or similar assessments online can help you determine what their skills are. It can also boost confidence and indicate what they each bring to the team!

4. Assess and then talk about it—whenever you assess someone, it's important that you speak about it with them. This will increase both your understanding of them and their self-awareness. This works well when you complete personality or strength-based assessments. It will allow them to get together with similar people while sharing an appreciation for the strengths of others within the team. It increases their general understanding of how they work and how

others work, which means that they are much more effective.

5. Foster engagement—sometimes, your staff members will be unsure of their own strengths. As a leader, it's your job to help uncover them. If you encourage them to engage in tasks and activities as well as the team, you will be able to uncover their strengths quickly.

6. Encourage all of your team members to acknowledge the strengths of others—foster an environment where encouraging other members of the team is the norm. Get them talking about each other's strengths, so they can determine who is the best fit for particular tasks and activities. This starts to build a more open and communicative workflow.

7. Use Gallup's StrengthsFinder—as a leader, you can utilize Gallup's online StrengthsFinder assessment. It will help you to discover your team member's top five talents. It's a great place to begin! You could then spend time discussing it to identify deeper, underlying values.

8. Apply the *Rule of Three*—we've already talked about the rule of three, but what we mean here is that you can use it when wording your questions. What do you look forward to at work? Or, what aspect of work do you want

to do more of? And what are the qualities you need to complete your favorite task at work?

9. Give them a try—when you're aware of their strengths, don't forget to allow your team members to try out their skills. Observe or assess them while completing tasks that require them to use those skills. This can help you gauge not only how good their strengths are but also what areas need to be improved upon. Identifying areas for improvement is just as important as strengths. It is how we grow and develop our team members.

10. Create an open culture—this is important on a business level, as each company needs to show they value their leaders and team members. They can assess their strengths and help their leaders develop. The leaders will then help the staff. This will increase job satisfaction, so let your employees come to you and discuss their tasks, strengths, and areas of growth freely. You can help them develop their career if you foster an open culture.

11. Learn from the past—past experiences make us who we are today, and it's important that you utilize them. Ask your team members direct questions, like, *what are your unique strengths?* Or, *what projects or experiences did you enjoy the most?* You can then dig deeper. Consider their biggest learnings that arose

from their experiences and talk about what they may have done differently. Sometimes, talking it over can implant the idea of what to do should a similar experience arise.

12. Host a team member story day—people enjoy hearing real-life stories, so getting together and discussing 'A day in the life of...' is a great idea. You could also make this longer by asking them to tell the story of what made them who they are today. That will give them an opportunity to include key events, milestones, barriers they've faced, and their accomplishments. They can sum up the things they've learned on their journey so far! This can be an inspiring experience for everyone, plus it helps you get to know your team members on a more personal—and fun —level.

Use the STAR method to understand the strengths of your team—you can ask your employees to use the STAR method to demonstrate their strengths:

- **Situation**—describe the situation and context. **Task**—describe the task they completed. **Actions**—describe the actions they took to complete the task
- **Result**—reflect on the result and how successful it was. Think about how this unveils strengths.

The more you know about each of your team members and their strengths, the easier it will be for you as a leader to assign tasks and responsibilities in an effective way. In the next chapter, we'll focus more on clarifying roles and responsibilities within your team.

CLARIFY ROLES AND RESPPONSIBILITIES

*A*s a leader, it's important that you establish roles and responsibilities within your team. Everything will flow if everyone is clear about their role and what they must do. The work will get done.

If roles and responsibilities are unclear, it can mean your team is unproductive. Everyone needs clarity—they need to know what to prioritize and when. If one person has the same job title as another, then the tasks they complete may be similar. However, a leader can assign further responsibilities based on the strengths of that particular employee or divide tasks based on competencies.

In this chapter, we'll focus on what leaders can do to establish roles and responsibilities within their organizations. We'll look at why it's important to clarify who does what, how to fix it when things are unclear, and how rigidly defined responsibilities can reduce motivation.

First, let's consider whether your team is suffering as a result of unclear roles and responsibilities...

DOES YOUR TEAM SUFFER FROM HAVING UNCLEAR ROLES AND RESPONSIBILITIES?

If so, there may be many implications for your team. Ask yourself the following questions:

1. Does it seem as if your team is doing a lot of work but is still not achieving its goals? *Your employees may not be doing the right kind of work. Therefore, they are wasting their time. It's important to stay focused on your end goal. Every task you do should be strategically linked to achieving it somehow.*

2. Are your employees duplicating work? *This is important to consider; often, we repeat work that has already been done. So, have a system in place to check! For example, if you want to know about something expenditure-related, rather than adding everything up manually, there may already be a report completed by the financial department. It may be as simple as giving them a call to find out the data you need. Also, if you have two people who do the same job, double-check who is doing what to prevent duplication.*

3. Are your employees ever confused about what they should be doing? *If they are confused about the tasks they are performing—and aren't clear on what they're aiming for—it can be difficult for them to complete tasks effectively.*

THE IMPORTANCE OF HAVING CLEAR ROLES AND RESPONSIBILITIES

It's important to ensure that your whole team has clear roles and responsibilities. If they don't, it can cause numerous issues for the business, such as:

- They may not understand how they fit into the team, which may make them feel distant. They won't feel a connection, and communication will suffer as a result.
- They may be wasting time because they're unsure what to do and how to do it. Tasks don't get completed as a result, and the team may be unable to meet deadlines.
- Your team members are unsure if they are doing their job well. The danger with this is that they won't learn what works and what doesn't. If roles and responsibilities are clear, staff will be able to measure progress and performance against the standards they are working towards.
- Your team members may be at odds with one another, leaving them feeling frustrated. This

may result in conflict within the team. With clear roles and responsibilities, each employee knows what they have to do, but without them, they may find tasks conflict or work is duplicated.

HOW RIGID RESPONSIBILITIES REDUCE MOTIVATION

While it's important that roles and responsibilities are clearly communicated, sometimes a leader can go too far. Flexibility is the key here... so a leader should never be too rigid, as it will impact your team members' motivation.

If you define your team's roles and responsibilities in too much detail, you're in danger of creating further problems. Your team members may not want to complete others' tasks if they do not align with their stated roles and responsibilities. One of the most impactful ways to motivate a team is to provide them with autonomy, so make sure that you're not tying them up in limitations. This simply puts barriers in their way.

An innovative and effective leader will always allow their team to have some freedom to control their work without feeling that they need to follow strict rules or instructions constantly. Doing so gets boring. If your staff is bored, they are not motivated. Hence why flexibility and creative thinking should be encouraged. It ultimately keeps your staff motivated!

HOW TO REMEDY YOUR TEAM MEMBERS BEING UNCLEAR ABOUT THEIR ROLES AND

RESPONSIBILITIES

If your team members are unclear regarding their roles and responsibilities, it's your job as their leader to fix it. Here are some ways you can do this:

Clarify the roles on your team and think about who is responsible for what. Then consider any responsibility gaps and look for tasks that are sometimes duplicated. It's your job to notice these gaps.

Fix the gaps. Once you've clarified roles, review the gaps and assign the roles to specific team members. Be clear, and state who is responsible for what. You should always reflect on the strengths of each of your team members when assigning tasks and consider who will do what best. You could even discuss this with your team at a team meeting and decide who will take the reins together.

Clarify team roles by creating a RACI:

- **Responsible**: who will be doing the work?
  Accountable: who is ultimately accountable for the work, or who will approve it? This will likely be you.
- **Consulted**: who will be consulted about the task so that they can have some input? This person could be inside or outside of the team.

- **Informed**: who should be informed about the outcome of the work (but not included in how the work is done)?

You can even create a list of the people within your team and assign roles for each specific task. There should only ever be one person who is listed as accountable. This can help you and your team clarify who is responsible for what.

Clarify the roles on your team by getting feedback. We've talked about open communication and asking your team for feedback on who is responsible for what and whether or not they are clear. You could ask them to recap what they need to do, or you could ask questions to clarify your understanding and theirs. This will improve performance, and it can also result in a greater sense of job satisfaction.

Clarify any unclear roles and responsibilities. It's ultimately up to you to track your team's work and prevent things from being overlooked. You could use a simple spreadsheet to help you keep track of your team's work and check in on their progress. Everyone on the team will begin to understand what work others are doing, especially when you're working in an open, communicative environment.

Communicate the roles and responsibilities of the team to clarify them. It's important that your team understands their roles and responsibilities and that stakeholders understand them as well... that includes your boss. If you don't do this, you're in danger of your team being asked to perform tasks that are out of alignment. This could cause further problems for you and them, as you will struggle to meet your goals and targets.

As a leader, you have the responsibility of assigning the roles and responsibilities to your team that help you achieve your team goals, which all contribute towards the business's goals. Everything has a purpose. It's important to make this super-clear to your team members. They need to know what they are aiming for, how they're contributing, and what they need to do to achieve the end goal. This will ensure your team is productive, aligned with the business, and has meaning.

To have purpose or meaning, you need to ensure you are clear on the goals you are striving towards. That's why, in the next chapter, we'll focus on syncing all goals!

19

SYNC ALL GOALS

*O*ur personal and team goals give us purpose, but only if they are in pursuit of something bigger—an end goal for the business. Your goals are your contribution to the vision or strategy of the organization, and that's why it's important that you understand how your team goals— and the goals you set for each team member—support that vision.

Imagine the organization's vision and goals sitting at the top. They are supported by groups of people— teams. The teams have their own goals, but they are supported by each individual person and their personal goals. Syncing goals means that everyone is working towards the same thing. That means the work performed by the team is harmonized. While your team is helping the overall business strategy, *how do we sync our goals effectively?*

In this chapter, we'll not only discuss the importance of aligning the goals of the organization, but we'll also review how you can align them with your team.

> *"If everyone is moving forward together, then success takes care of itself."*
> ~ Henry Ford

If goals are synced, everyone can move forward together for the betterment of themselves, our teams, and our company!

ALIGNMENT WITHIN THE ORGANIZATION

Alignment within the organization is the biggest difference between whether a company is high-performing or low-performing. LSA Global research found that companies grow 58% faster if they are highly aligned, and 72% are more profitable. This means they outperform their unaligned peers when it comes to customer satisfaction, customer retention, leadership, and employee engagement. This contributes to businesses being more successful overall.

To really align, individual, team, and business goals must all sync. Everything contributes to the end goal, which is the overall purpose of everything! The main benefits of ensuring that goals are aligned throughout the organization are:

1. Organizational strategies are formed from goals, they set the tone

2. Employees recognize how they contribute towards the team and organizational goals
3. The priorities of the team and business are clarified
4. Employees and teams are connected through aligned goals

Clearly, there are many benefits to aligning goals. Now we'll talk about how an organization can ensure this happens. It takes a whole-employee approach, which starts at the very top!

HOW CAN WE ALIGN GOALS THROUGHOUT THE WHOLE ORGANIZATION?

Goal setting is big in every organization, but in order to ensure alignment throughout, goals must align with one another. When it comes to ensuring all goals align throughout the organization, you must:

Set organizational goals that are clear. For alignment to occur, everyone must be onboard because it begins at the top. The company vision and strategies need to be produced so that it's possible for each team to align. You then need to make sure that you and your team are super-clear on your objectives. It's much easier to understand goals and visions that are clear and have a purpose. Get other leaders and management to buy into your goals. Leadership needs to be involved at this stage, so it's important that senior and middle management meet up to discuss the vision, strategies, benchmarks, and goals that have been identified for the organization. The leaders and managers can give feedback in relation to this. For alignment to occur, it's important that the company listens to any questions or feedback. This will increase alignment as everyone is working together. Communicate goals to everyone, on every level.

Goals must be communicated on all levels so that everyone can become accountable and therefore feel more inclined to meet them. Less than half of employees within an organization report that they know what their company's goals are. Discussing goals regularly—with everyone in the organization—connects it with its initiative and this helps to reinforce them.

Help other employees to accomplish their goals. As a leader, you also need to be there to support your team to reach its goals. In most cases, you will not only set them for your team members but will also encourage them to take ownership of their goals in order to succeed. It's important that you understand the roles of the individual contributors within your team, as well as the company's goals. You may need to offer training and development to help employees succeed, as well as attend meetings and one-to-ones that allow time to discuss any potential issues or misalignment. If an employee has support, they are more likely to stay aligned with strategies and achieve their goals or even surpass them.

Alignment is the key to success for the organization.

So, engage with leadership and help your team members understand what is expected of them and how their work fits into the bigger picture. Aligned goals create an atmosphere in which everyone works together because everyone understands their role. It's up to you and the business to put your company at an advantage by ensuring everything is aligned.

20

THE LEADER AS A COACH

*Y*ou'll find that, in your role as a leader, you have many hats. Sometimes you need to be a friend, a confidante, an advisor or counselor, a problem-solver, a mentor, and a manager. And you'll do all of this while still maintaining your role as a professional, effective, and well-respected leader. The world of coaching is a flourishing industry right now, and many innovative leaders are finding that they need to become coaches. This can be a positive thing because coaching and leading work hand-in-hand. Not only does this develop your skills as a leader, but it also pushes your staff to embrace and take ownership of their own development.

This chapter will guide you on how to utilize your leadership skills and develop them to become an influential coach within your organization. We'll now look at how the role of the manager is becoming coach-orientated; we'll explore different coaching styles, and review coaching in an organizational capacity to ensure it's the right fit for you, your team, and the organization.

If you really want to stand out and excel as a leader, this chapter is for you!

THE MANAGER BECOMING COACH-ORIENTATED

There's no doubt that the role of a manager is changing, but *did you know it's becoming more coach-orientated?* You may be wondering what that means exactly. It's really quite simple to explain...

An effective manager who takes a coach-orientated approach:

Doesn't give you the answers to your problems, instead, they ask questions so that you can discover your own answers and form your own path Refrains from judgment, but offers you support as necessary

Does not dictate training and development, but facilitates this based on your needs

You see, someone who coaches others is an enabler. They enable people to follow their own dreams and support them in getting to where they need to be. This promotes creative thinking and encourages the employee to be accountable for their own actions and development.

COACHING STYLES

When you coach your team members, there are different styles you can use to help you support them effectively. We're going to explore four styles in this chapter: directive, laissez-faire, non-directive, and situational.

1. **Directive coaching**—uses a 'show and tell' approach, where the coach shows, explains and demonstrates what needs to be done and how. It should be used when a new employee has joined the team. It should now, however, be overused, as it disempowers the employee's own learning journey.

2. **Laissez-faire coaching**—this is when you leave your team members to find the right approach themselves and manage their own work, as they are already productive. This means coaching isn't really necessary at all, so you can take a step back and allow them to get on with it. *A good coach is able to recognize when NOT to coach as much as when TO coach.*

3. **Non-directive coaching**—for this method, you must be able to withhold your judgment and simply listen and ask questions of your team members. You will draw insight, creativity, and wisdom from your employees, and help them cope with and overcome their

own challenges. This will fill the individual with energy and confidence as they have figured it out themselves. It's not always easy for a manager to take a step back and ensure they are not providing the answers; instead, are enabling their staff to do so. This can be very powerful when used correctly.

4. **Situational coaching**—a balanced approach to coaching. It links to the directive and non-directive coaching. You'll choose which method to use based on the specific situation, the challenge faced, and the needs of the employee. This means that if there is a need for you to tell your staff what to do, you use directive coaching, but if it's something you know they can deal with, it's a case of using non-directive methods. Tapping into both methods is super-supportive and helpful for your staff as it helps them to develop at a pace, they are comfortable with.

The diagram below can help you understand the different methods, and the details on the left indicate what information you need to put in as the coach. The information along the bottom details the energy your employee will feel due to that particular coaching method. Sometimes, it's simply about striking the right balance.

Styles of Coaching

More info put in	1. Directive	4. Situational
Less info put in	2. Laissez-faire	3. Nondirective
	Less energy pulled out	More energy pulled out

HOW CAN I ENSURE COACHING IS THE RIGHT FIT FOR ME AND FOR MY ORGANIZATION?

IT'S NOT enough to simply teach leaders and managers to coach better. For coaching to really make a difference, it needs to be adopted in a capacity that fits within your company culture. Sometimes, that means changes need to be made to create a cultural transformation. To do this, you can:

Explain the 'why'—when you work in a busy environment, managers and professionals may see coaching as being the latest trend, which means they may not take it seriously. That's why you must make it clear how valuable it is for the organization, its leaders and managers, and its employees. Coaching maximizes the skills of the workforce, motivates staff, helps them to problem-solve, and encourages them to take charge of their own development. It's a great way to gain fresh insights and improve how we deal with clients! Let everyone know how it aligns with the business to get them onboard.

You do it!—if you want others to embrace coaching, you must model it. Modeling is a common teaching technique. Others see you do something, and notice how successful it is, so they want a piece of the action! If your team becomes the top-performing team—and you can link aspects of this to your coaching—others will follow your lead, and higher management will be on board with this as well. Model the benefits of adopting a coaching culture within your forward-thinking organization.

Break down the barriers—sometimes, there are organizational barriers to creating a coaching culture among leaders and managers. Often, leaders and employees are reluctant to try something new for fear that it will not work, and time will be wasted. The whole culture would need to make a shift into a learning culture, in which the managers ask coaching questions... such as, what's working? What's not working? How can we support you? What are you trying to do, and what do you think is a better choice? Again, it isn't always easy to get higher management on board, so model it within your team first and deliver feedback to leaders and management about your successes and progress.

Reinventing leaders and managers as coaches can draw out creativity, energy, and learning, while enabling all staff to be responsible and accountable for their work and development (to a certain extent). Businesses that want to prosper in the future must adopt new ways of working and become adaptable to change. Remember, you are a powerful and influential female figure who absolutely can drive this forward.

To finalize this section, we'll be discussing the

importance of building trust within your team. Everything you've learned so far leads to this because if there is no trust - there is no team!

21

NO TRUST - NO TEAM

*W*ithout trust, there is no team. For teamwork to be effective, you all must work together to achieve goals. You can only do this if you trust each other!

> "Great teams have trust at the heart of their success. If you don't trust each other, you'll play safe. Trust makes it possible to aim higher. To leap further and to know someone has your back if you fall."
> ~ Adam Grant

This chapter covers the dimensions of trust and how to build trust amongst your team members. We'll also be exploring the three dimensions of trust, and how you can build it in the workplace as a leader. While this isn't always the simplest of tasks, it is worthwhile.

So, before we continue, let's examine why trust is so important for your team...

WHY IS TRUST SO IMPORTANT FOR MY TEAM?

It's likely that, in your role, situations have occurred in which one of your team members hasn't performed to your expectations. Maybe you want to delegate a task to them but feel hesitant because of previous experience. The employee may even be hardworking and likable, but you are unsure if they are up to handling an important project. If you feel hesitant when it comes to delegating to them, it is because you don't have faith in them...

Can you trust this person to get the job done?

A core reason not to delegate is a lack of trust. Whether you're dealing with one employee or an entire team, trust is crucial in order for you to lead effectively. You must build trust with them... and keep it! Things can become unnecessarily complicated if you don't trust them or if they don't trust you.

The point is it's important for your team to function in the most effective way. Trust leads to speedy decision-making and innovative teamwork that ensures goals are met, and expectations can be exceeded.

THE THREE DIMENSIONS OF TRUST

Trust is said to revolve around 3 key areas. If we lack trust in a person's *capabilities*, we may not think they have the relevant skills to be able to complete tasks. If we lack trust in a person's *character*, we simply don't trust that they will complete the assigned tasks (this can be really problematic). If we lack trust in our *communication*, we may struggle when it comes to teamwork because we do not feel comfortable communicating worries and concerns or asking questions when we are unsure.

But what if you, as a leader, build trust in these areas?

Let's look at the benefits:

1. **Trust in capabilities** allows team members to make a difference by contributing their knowledge. Leveraging the skills of your team means that team members begin to tap into each other's knowledge by engaging more, being involved in decision-making, and teaching one another new skills. This builds trust as it shows employees are willing to support one another while also valuing their opinions. This can encourage organizations and teams to become competitive.

2. **Trust in character** represents each individual and is the starting point of team relationships, which are often mutually serving as you aim for the same goal. Intentions are often set here, along with the

direction of the teamwork and the tone. Each team member can build trust within the team when they do what they've promised. Doing so proves they are reliable.

3. **Trust in communication**—we need communication if we are to collaborate with others, as this often fuels our ability to work effectively with them. The more employees work together and communicate with each other, the more likely they are to accomplish their goals and be successful. Communication helps to build a bond, which means the team will have each other's backs and be able to work through issues together. This also makes us feel more comfortable when we make mistakes because we feel we're in a safe environment, which piggybacks on psychological safety. Trust is everything. It's the glue that holds all teams together.

When trust is achieved across those three dimensions, it's easier to have honest conversations with our team. Once the team develops strong bonds, everyone can have productive conversations about performance. As a leader, you can address issues and resolve problems quickly while supporting the team because the trust you've built demonstrates how much you care about them, so they know you're looking out for their best interests. *But... how can you build trust within your team?* We'll explore that next...

HOW TO BUILD TRUST IN THE WORKPL ACE

There are nine strategies that you can use if you want to foster a trustful environment at work. We'll look at each of them in turn:

1. Ensure you listen more than you speak—your employees are people. People want to express their unique opinions and ideas. Make sure you listen when they speak and encourage them to talk to you. This builds positive relationships between team members and helps to install mutual trust.
2. Make sure you act on the feedback you receive— while a leader can't be everywhere at all times; it's important that they take on valuable feedback and respond to it. If you want to build trust, you should encourage your employees to voice their opinions. You have to acknowledge and act on this to be effective. Many employees stop giving feedback because they feel it's only going to be ignored and is, therefore, a waste of time. Be different! Build trust with your employees.
3. Be appreciative—feeling appreciated is a key motivator at work. While yes, we get paid to

KARINA G. SANCHEZ

work, actually feeling valued makes a difference in how an employee performs a task. We've talked about praise already in this book, but ensure you build a sense of community by simply saying 'thank you'. 9 out of 10 employees report that they feel higher levels of trust in their boss when they have been recognized or thanked for their work. It confirms they are doing a good job, and it makes them feel good.

4. Put your trust in your team to empower them — there are many occasions when a leader has to lead by example. If you take the first step by placing trust in your employees, they are more likely to reciprocate. You can do this by encouraging their professional development, giving them opportunities or responsibilities, or allowing them to come to a meeting that they would not usually attend. This aids development, and nobody likes to be micromanaged as it reduces motivation and suggests to your employees that you don't believe they can complete their tasks effectively. Trust cannot be built on this basis, as these actions suggest a lack of trust.

5. Coach and encourage your team—we've discussed the leader's coaching responsibilities in the previous chapter, so remember, you play a vital role in developing your staff and building trust within your organization. Authentic leadership

undoubtedly cultivates trust. So, rather than acting like a 'bossy' boss and chastising your staff when you feel they have underperformed, instead coach them. Give them advice, ask the right questions to help them problem-solve, and guide them if necessary.

6. Be consistent—when you're a leader, you must follow up your words with actions. Show up every day, and practice what you preach. Make your expectations clear and follow any standards you set. Being consistent shows that you are trustworthy and encourages your staff to work to a higher standard. It also increases your confidence in leadership!

7. Recognize the importance of soft skills and non-verbal communication—they are both equally powerful and say a lot about a person. While verbal communication is important, you can demonstrate your feelings, your level of engagement, and your interest, by nodding, altering your voice tone, using hand gestures, and maintaining eye contact. Positive body language shows our human side; it shows that we are genuine and feel warm, excited, or empathetic about the situation. Speaking from the heart embraces the real you, and you should never pretend to be something you're not.

8. You must have an inclusive culture—we've discussed inclusivity a lot in this book, and you must remember that a dysfunctional culture prevents the organization from meeting its goals. Inclusivity ensures that all employees feel valued and accepted. When there are promotional opportunities, equal pay, and staff benefits for all, all staff feel valued and are often happier at work. A diverse organization brings together a range of people and skills, all with different experiences, which enriches the culture. Inclusivity helps to build trust as it promotes acceptance.

9. Honesty is the best policy—the truth is vitally important, even though it's sometimes difficult. We all like to help and serve others, and honesty builds trust and respect. You should never make promises to your team members that you are unable to keep, and while you remain sensitive to their feelings, you owe it to them to be professional. It's a good idea to keep your team updated on everything that has to do with the business, which means being as transparent as possible. If major changes are occurring and you haven't informed your team—but it's apparent you knew before they did—you can lose their trust.

When trust is lost, it's difficult to reclaim.

Trust is important to start building with your team members today. As a leader, it's up to you to act... now! The foundation of an effective team is dependent on trust, as it is a determining factor of how well that team will perform. As a new leader, it's important that you work on building trust quickly and efficiently, so you can begin shaping your top-performing team.

Always remember, you are a leader because you deserve to be. You already have amazing skills, and now it's your turn to help your team excel. Everything begins with trust...

As we move to the end of section III, remember to head over to section IV. It has all the extra tools you need to master your leadership skills.

It's your time to begin!

SECTION IV – EXTRA TOOLS & RESOURCES

While you have all the information you need to excel as a leader, it's important that you also feel fully equipped to deal with any situation that arises. You're here now because you are the next super successful leader, and you are going to take the world by storm using your new, fresh, charismatic leadership style! It is one that not only gets results but paves the way for the next generation of leaders. You are the beginning of a revolution in leadership!

In this section, you'll be provided with the tools you need to find out your leadership style, and you'll be prepared with powerful coaching questions you can use today. You'll also work through templates and plans to ensure you are ready to set expectations, create development plans, improve performance, and correct behavior that lasts.

> *"The quality of a leader is reflected in the standards they set for themselves."*
> ~ Ray Kroc

As a leader, it's your time to set the standards for yourself and others!

22

YOUR LEADERSHIP STYLE
FINDER

here are 10 common leadership styles. In this chapter, we'll look at them more closely. *What type of leader are you?*

Coaching style

You may be a coaching leader if you value learning for growth purposes, support your employees, and would rather offer guidance than make demands. You are also self-aware, enjoy using guided questions, and always balance providing information with helping others find their answers.

The benefits of being a coaching leader are that they promote free-thinking and career development and empower their staff. You are therefore seen as an inspiring, valuable leader within the organization. If you are a coaching leader, you'll find that this can be time-consuming, as you need to spend a considerable amount of time with your employees on a one-to-one basis, so incorporating this style 30% of the time, allows you to balance your tasks.

Visionary Style

A visionary leader is inspirational, innovative, and optimistic. They work in a strategic way, and yet their confidence allows them to take risks. They have a magnetic personalities and are often described as being persistent and bold.

Visionary leaders are sometimes so focused on the bigger picture that they miss opportunities and important details, which means their team members sometimes feel unheard. This is something you can look to remedy. The benefits of being a visionary leader are that you help bring teams together, improve outdated company practices, and aid with business growth.

Servant Style

This style of leadership is very people-oriented. The leader primarily focuses on what the team wants, personally and professionally. This ensures they produce outstanding work, perform it effectively, and are most productive. If your team respects you, can communicate well, and motivates them... well, you could be a servant leader. If so, you will really care about your employees and feel committed to helping them grow professionally. You'll also encourage them to collaborate and engage.

Servant leaders are excellent at motivating staff so that they become top performers. They will ensure their team members are excellent decision-makers, trustful in their team, productive, and loyal. This type of leader is excellent at developing the leaders of tomorrow. Still, sometimes they can feel burnt out because of their level of responsibility and find it difficult to show their authority.

Autocratic Style

If you are focused on competence and outcomes, then you could be an autocratic-style leader. They are authoritative figures who often make decisions alone and provide clear direction to their employees. They are self-motivated, confident, and always follow the rules. They are highly dependable and regularly communicate in a concise, clear way. They enjoy structure and like to supervise their direct reports.

Autocratic-style leaders drive productivity and reduce any stress that their team members feel due to their ability to make quick decisions. Such leaders often feel responsible for everything that happens, resulting in stress. They can also be inflexible and closed off to the ideas of others, so if this is you... then one of the things you may need to pay attention to is your willingness to honor the work-life balance.

Autocratic leaders can find themselves quickly burnt out.

Laissez-faire style

Laissez-faire style and autocratic leaders are polar opposites, as they look to provide very little—or no supervision to their employees whatsoever. If you can delegate effectively, only take control when needed, and offer constructive criticism while providing proficient resources and tools, you may be a laissez-faire leader. This style of leader tends to promote an autonomous work environment and helps their team foster leadership skills and qualities.

While this style is not always suitable for new employees who may need extra guidance, support, and training, laissez-faire leaders can often create a relaxed work environment, have a high staff retention rate, and encourage their direct reports to be accountable for their actions and development.

Democratic style

This leadership style demonstrates that you value your team by including them in decisions and group discussions while promoting an environment where everyone can share their ideas and opinions. A democratic leader can resolve conflict easily and remains flexible. They consider the opinions of others, including their team, and are open to receiving feedback.

The democratic leader boosts morale and empowers their staff. As employees are part of their decision-making, they know what they need to do. Therefore, these leaders don't need to monitor progress closely. Sometimes this leadership style is inefficient, and if you have a member of staff who doesn't like to share their ideas publicly, they could feel pressured by this approach.

Pacesetting style

Pacesetting leaders achieve results fast. They find themselves focused on performance. They set high standards and are excellent at motivating others and holding their team accountable. If you are goal-focused, have high standards, and value increasing performance above all else, you could be a pacesetting leader. If so, you will be willing to roll your sleeves up and help the team achieve goals if the situation calls for it.

While pacesetting leaders push employees to achieve goals, they are often slow at praising others. This can demotivate. Their team can feel stressed out, and the fast-paced working environment can mean that there is a lack of clarity. They are excellent at promoting dynamic work environments and injecting energy into their staff.

Transformational style

If you are inspiring, encouraging, and often reflect

on the big picture, you could be a transformational leader. This leadership style focuses on goal setting, improved employee motivation, and clear communication. They are committed to organizational objectives and have formed mutual respect with their team. They are creative, and they do not partake in constant supervision when leading their team.

This type of leadership is ethical and goal-orientated. Such leaders value personal connections with their teams, which boosts employee retention and morale. Sometimes, individuals under them may feel overlooked, as if their wins go unnoticed as they focus on the transformation rather than the milestones achieved.

Transactional Style

This is someone who values corporate structure and is both pragmatic and practical while believing that authority should not be questioned. They love to hit goals but can, at times, be reactionary. They also micromanage while focusing on performance, goals, and incentives.

The benefits of being a transactional style leader are: Being excellent at achieving goals and also helping others do so. Sometimes, people who lead like this are known to get caught up in short-term goals, limit creativity, and demotivate employees. If this is your style, remember to remember the long-term goals, so you don't lose sight of them!

Bureaucratic style

You're a bureaucratic leader if you are strong-willed, self-disciplined, and detail-oriented. While you focus on the tasks at hand, you have a great work ethic and really value structure and adherence to rules in the workplace. You are committed and expect your team to follow the rules.

This type of leadership is efficient, and the teams can often meet targets and goals easily. However, this type of leader may struggle to create close personal bonds with team members. They may restrict the creativity of some employees and sometimes struggle with change.

WHICH TYPE OF LEADER ARE YOU?

You must dig deep and consider which leadership style is most appropriate for you. You can think through the following questions:

1. *Do I like to make decisions alone, or do I like to receive input?*
2. *Do I value goals or relationships more in the workplace? Are short or long-term goals more important to me?*
3. *Do I like structure, or do I prefer a more flexible approach? What does the ideal team dynamic look like to me?*

4. *Do I prefer to empower others or give them direction?*

Really consider your answers here and determine which leadership category fits you best. Use the information to work on your development areas and challenges while utilizing your leadership strengths.

23

---

70 POWERFUL COACHING QUESTIONS

*W*hile we've already spoken about how it's a good idea for a leader to embrace coaching, you must also be able to ask the right questions. To help you prepare, we've created 70 powerful coaching questions to help you begin your coaching journey.

Previously, you may have heard of the GROW model. It is a very common framework used in coaching. GROW is an acronym - Goal, Reality (current), Options, Will (way forward). The questions we'll cover below stem from this framework. Remember, when asking these questions, take it slow and allow thinking time before expecting your employees to respond.

Goals

The first 10 questions to help you gain clarity when it comes to goals:

1. What do you hope to accomplish from today's discussion?
2. What would that be if you had to choose one goal to achieve?
3. What do you want to happen with (situation/task)?
4. What is it that you really want?
5. What result are you aiming for?
6. What would you like to achieve?
7. If you could change something, what would it be?
8. What outcome is ideal for you?
9. Why do you want this outcome or to achieve this goal?
10. What are the benefits if you achieve your goal?

Reality

The next 20 questions focus on the current reality you are in and will help you gain clarity:

1. What is happening now and what is happening as a result (think about cause and effect – who, what, when, and how often)?
2. What steps have you taken already toward reaching your goal?

3. Tell me, what did you do (describe it)?
4. Do you think you're on track to achieve your goal?
5. Where are you now, on a scale of 1-10?
6. Tell me, what progress have you made so far?
7. What do you think has contributed to your success so far?
8. What is working for you?
9. What exactly is required of you?
10. What has stopped you from hitting your goal already?
11. Why do you think that is?
12. What do you think was really happening?
13. Who else has achieved that particular goal?
14. What have you learned so far?
15. What methods have you tried already?
16. Do you think you can turn this around?
17. What could you do better?
18. If you asked (another team member), what do you think they would say about you/this?
19. How would you respond if someone said or did [this]?
20. How severe, serious, or urgent is the situation on a scale of 1-10?

Options

When you understand your reality, you'll have a clearer understanding of the situation. This means you can explore it further by reviewing your options. This will help you consider solutions. The next 20 questions will help you explore options:

1. What options do you have?
2. What do you think your next steps should be?
3. What should be your first step?
4. What could you do better to ensure you get the result you want?
5. What else could you have done?
6. Is there anyone else who might be able to help you?
7. If you do nothing, what will happen?
8. What has worked for you in the past, and how do you think you could do more of that?
9. If you did that, what do you think would happen?
10. What part are you finding the most difficult?
11. If you were advising a friend, what would you tell them?
12. What do you have to gain or lose by doing or saying that?
13. What do you think would happen if someone said or did that to you?
14. What is the best or worst thing that could happen in relation to that option?
15. Which option would you opt for right now if you had to choose?
16. How would you approach this, based on your previous experience in similar situations?
17. Is there anything you could do differently?

18. Do you know anyone who has encountered a situation like this one?
19. What would you do if anything was possible?
20. Is there anything else you would do?

Will

The final 20 questions focus on will (this is your way forward), as this is the final step in the GROW model. The aim of this is to help your employees create a plan of action so they know how to move forward or resolve the problem at hand:

1. How are you going to move forward?
2. What do you think you need to do immediately?
3. Could you explain how you'll do that?
4. How will you know when you've completed it?
5. What else could you do?
6. Do you think your plan is likely to succeed? On a scale of 1-10, what's the likelihood?
7. What would make this increase to 10?
8. What barriers are preventing you from achieving success?
9. What plans do you need to make, or what roadblocks do you expect to encounter?
10. Are there any resources that can help you?
11. What's missing?

12. If you take one small step now, where will you be?
13. When do you plan on starting?
14. If you are successful, how will you know?
15. If you want to get that done, what support will you need?
16. What would happen if you did not do this? What is the cost (time/money etc.)?
17. What do you need from others to ensure you achieve this?
18. What three actions can you take this week to head toward your goal?
19. On a scale of 1-10, how motivated or committed are you to getting this done?
20. How can you make it 10?

These questions are probing, so you can help your employees resolve any issues, overcome barriers, and get started on their tasks. Conversations don't have to be neat... they have to be thought-provoking! Eventually, they will flow better and feel more natural. Remember, practice makes perfect.

24

EXPECTATION SETTING

*A*s a leader, it's important that you set expectations with your employees in the clearest way possible. Having clear expectations benefits the business and its staff, as productivity and performance increase when everyone knows what's expected of them.

Setting expectations

If you want to set expectations for your staff, there are five things you need to figure out to do so effectively:

What are the employees' expectations? The organization will have set expectations for its employees. For example, they may need to display a positive attitude, be honest, be respectful, complete their work to high standards, follow policies and procedures, and conduct themselves in a professional manner at all times. In return, your employee will also have expectations. These include expecting to be treated fairly, receiving training support and leadership, being paid on time, working in safe environments, receiving regular feedback on performance, and being informed about job responsibilities and policies, and procedures.

What are the team's expectations? While team expectations are similar to individual ones, they are different. Every team member should be accountable for team goals, which are necessary to ensure cohesive working practices and productivity. Team expectations are usually based on behaviors within that team. For example, being accountable for your work, being flexible, respecting each other, asking for help or feedback as necessary, and ensuring you work in a safe environment. As a leader, you need to be aware of all of these expectations, so you can help your team members meet them. You lead by example.

What are performance expectations? You need to think about how your employees are meant to perform, so think about what they need to achieve and be specific. Performance expectations allow you to move forward toward company goals and can be used to monitor progress. To set performance expectations, inform your team members of the goal you want to achieve. Use SMART goals and set objectives to ensure your employees know how they can achieve them and what they need to do. In essence, you will provide the map, and they will follow.

How do you communicate and manage expectations? Ensure you communicate and manage expectations clearly. It's a good idea to meet with your employees and ensure you give them a chance to ask questions and seek guidance. Make sure you are reachable, just in case they have a question later, and be sure to explain the importance of these expectations. Having one-on-one meetings and regularly discussing ongoing projects and development opportunities is good. Make sure you highlight any goals in a clear and simple format. You could do this during a meeting or over email. Then manage progress by checking in with your team members or by asking them to update you (daily, weekly, bi-weekly, or monthly—depending on the project).

A STEP-BY-STEP GUIDE TO SETTING EXPECTATIONS FOR YOUR TEAM

Steps you can take to set expectations for new and existing staff members:

- Determine your expectations—write a list of realistic expectations for your staff. Really think about this and be careful not to demand too much. Keep them achievable and fair.
- Reduce confusion by clarifying your expectations—we've already talked through this. Help your employees set goals and have open discussions while also addressing

questions. Always ensure they fully understand your expectations.

- Inform team members why the expectations are important—it's one thing to explain what a person must do, but the important thing is to explain the 'why' behind it. By telling them why and stressing the importance, you will motivate them as they will see the big picture and understand how they contribute to the company.
- Give examples that show why expectations are important - doing this can help your staff understand. For example, maintaining a positive attitude reduces stress and increases morale.

Another example would be working in a timely fashion, which ensures operations run effortlessly and we stay on schedule.

- Gain commitments and agreements—get your employees to sign off on these expectations. They are more likely to follow through if they are committed to them and agree with them. This, in turn, will give them a sense of accomplishment and accountability.

You're now ready to set clear expectations for your direct reports and will be able to do so confidently.

25

INDIVIDUAL DEVELOPMENT
PLAN (IDP)

*A*n individual development plan is a tool that all successful leaders use to help employees develop and grow. It can help them focus on their career goals and their performance, as well as keep them motivated.

An individual development plan is an agreement between you and your employees. It details how they will improve their performance. This is customized to meet the needs of the employee, and it should include the details of any skills the employee wants to learn. It is an action plan that lays out strengths, weaknesses, and goals.

WHAT IS AN INDIVIDUAL LEARNING PL AN?

Plans are much more effective—and simpler—when

you follow a template, so take a look at the step-by-step plan below of the things you should include:

1. **Professional goals**—do they want a promotion/career development?
2. **Aspirations**—what projects do they want to be involved in, or what do they aspire to be/do?
3. **Talents and strengths**—what are their core competencies, skills, and talents? What positive feedback addresses these strengths, and how positive do they feel?
4. **Opportunities for development**—what opportunities may arise for them to improve? Work shadowing or training, for example.
5. **An action plan** (with goals)—what goals are you working towards, and how will you reach them? Set an end goal and then work backward to work out the steps you will take to get from where the person is now, to where they want to be.

An individual development plan is a useful tool because it allows you to monitor progress and ensure you have fulfilled certain steps. It can also ensure that you understand your strengths while observing potential areas for improvement.

HOW TO IMPLEMENT AN INDIVIDUAL DEVELOPMENT PLAN

In order to implement an individual development plan, arrange one-to-one meetings with each of your employees, then develop your own plan that will encourage conversations with them to be effective.

Begin with your own plan. Think about how your manager encouraged you to make improvements. Assess yourself in an honest way. Next, get ready for the conversations you'll be having with your team members. Remember to cover all the points in the step-by-step plan above.

It's up to you, as their leader, to help them add substance to their plan. Consider these questions to get your juices flowing:

1. What can your team members accomplish while carrying out everyday responsibilities?
2. Can your company spare time and money to allow them time to complete these development opportunities? If so, how much can be spared?
3. Have you included action steps—that are specific and measurable—to enable you to monitor progress?
4. How will this benefit both the employee and the company?

Once you know what is feasible and realistic, you can really consider how they can achieve their goals. Ensure you're clear on how they will benefit the organization as well as the individual.

DEVELOPMENT PL AN TEMPL ATE

A development plan will include the following information:

Employee name:
Job role, function, and job title:
Location:
Date:
Professional goals and aspirations: Strengths and talents:
Development opportunities:
Action plan (goals or steps):
Step or action:
Schedule:
Cost and conditions:

DEVELOPMENT PLAN EXAMPLE

Employee name: *Diane Williams*

Job role, function, job title: *Sales and Marketing, executing marketing campaigns on social media, Marketing Assistant*

Location: *Los Angeles*
Date: *12/12/2022*
Professional goals and aspirations:

1. *Advancement into a leadership role*

2. *Excel in current role and take on more responsibilities for the next marketing campaign*
Strengths and talents:

Organizational skills Meeting deadlines Communication skills Creative thinking **Development opportunities**:

1. *Job-shadow others with more experience, including your leader, to learn about their roles and responsibilities*
2. *Take the lead when the leader is unavailable and keep the leader updated on progress via email*
3. *Exceed minimum expectations by creating high-quality, engaging content that converts to sales*

Action plan (goals or steps):

- **Step or action**: *Research the customers that your business products appeal to, and aim to increase engagement on your social media marketing campaign by 50%*
- **Schedule**: *Run the marketing campaign for 4 weeks across three channels—Facebook, LinkedIn, and Instagram*
- **Cost and conditions**: *Achieve a 20% improvement in conversion rates without increasing the company's marketing budget for this project.*

INDIVIDUAL DEVELOPMENT PLAN FAQS

1. How is an individual development plan different from a performance review? A performance review looks at the person's performance in their current role, but a development plan looks at how they can develop and grow in relation to their career development.

2. How do examples from an individual development plan differ from a personal development plan? There isn't necessarily a difference, but some organizations prefer to call them one or the other.

3. Why should I create an individual development plan? It shows that, as a leader, you are there to help your employees develop and grow in a professional capacity! It demonstrates that you are invested in them and your company—this level of investment results in higher levels of productivity.

4. Should individual development plans be compulsory? If they are new, it's best to discuss your plans with employees, so they don't feel singled out. Often people are skeptical when reviewing their own performance, and it may cause anxiety.

26

PERFORMANCE IMPROVEMENT PLAN (PIP)

a Performance Improvement Plan is a Tool typically used only if an employee is performing poorly. It is their chance to improve and make changes. It ensures there are clear goals and objectives to aid improvement. As a leader, it's often your job to implement it if necessary. *But what exactly is a performance improvement plan?*

WHAT IS A PERFORMANCE IMPROVEMENT PL AN?

This document details where your direct report needs to make improvements and what that will involve. It will detail training and skills that the employee needs, and it should include clear goals and next steps that the employee will need to complete to maintain their current employment or role. The plan itself can be adapted. So, while it can be used when serious improvements need to be made, it can also be used to address minor issues.

THE PURPOSE AND BENEFITS OF A PERFORMANCE IMPROVEMENT PL AN

PIPs are often used to resolve poor performance issues, as a way to retain an employee while attempting to get them to rectify the problem. Of course, there are many benefits to this, including:

1. It creates a better culture in the company— the company responds in a more positive way by trying to help staff improve and promote accountability. This is clearly better than simply letting go or reprimanding their employees for their performance. It can make your team members feel more valued.
2. It saves both money and time—high turnover is very expensive and takes a lot of time, so it's much easier to develop, support, and retain the employees you already have. This is a more cost-effective and better use of time. Consider the recruitment process and the training required for new staff members… then you'll realize why it's much more efficient! On average it takes anywhere from six months to one year for a new employee to become comfortable in their role

and in the hundreds of thousands in recruitment costs.

3. It's more effective than a review—generally, performance reviews are done at the end of the year, whereas a personal improvement plan can be put in place any time it's needed as it's much more focused. Employees don't always react well to feedback—or may even believe that you are plain wrong—so PIPs are useful as they are clear and focused. Employees see where they need to improve as the steps are clearly outlined. This allows them to feel encouraged to do better.

AN EXAMPLE OF A PERFORMANCE IMPROVE-MENT PLAN

First, it's important to have a conversation with your employee and draw up a draft plan. It then needs to be reviewed by HR, for agreement.

Here is an example of how you may look to improve the quality of your work. It's recommended to establish:

1. **A goal**—the goal is to improve your quality of work (you can be more specific here when working with your employees) **Objectives**—these are the steps you'll take to achieve your goals, and deadlines are important here as well. If you want to improve the quality of

your work, your objective might be to produce work that includes the correct information and is free of errors.

2. **Action**—you must complete the action by the agreed date. i.e. Produce work that includes the correct information and is free of errors.

3. **Metrics**—they are used to measure your performance, so if you are late meeting a deadline or the quality of your work is not up to the standard agreed upon, your metrics will be lower.

HOW TO WRITE A PERFORMANCE IMPROVEMENT PL AN

Now you have the relevant information, it's time to put it all together and write your plan. You can follow the steps below:

Decide what is acceptable performance—you must inform your employees of what you expect, so let them know what is acceptable when it comes to their performance. Be sure to inform your employee what to expect from the meeting beforehand... don't simply pull out a document and begin discussing problems! Both of you need to provide input and be committed to the cause.

What measurable objective can be set? You will have to determine the objectives that your employee should meet in order to make improvements. You can use the SMART framework for this. It's important to try and find out what the root cause of the matter is, as this can help to determine how to improve. You have to pinpoint the problem before you can resolve it.

Define the support you will offer your employee— really consider how you can help your staff member reach their PIP goal. Maybe you will be required to train or coach your staff member along the way to help them build confidence. Support will encourage them to succeed!

Schedule meetings to check in on progress— ensure you agree on how often you will meet and put this in your calendar. Send them a quick email to remind them about the meeting and see how they are getting on. This way, your team members will get a chance to communicate any issues they are having as they arise.

Make the consequences clear—it's important that you inform your employees of potential consequences if they do not make the relevant improvements. Even so, try to make this positive by letting them know what they do well, and ensure they sign the PIP to demonstrate their commitment to the process.

WHAT IS THE BEST WAY TO RESPOND TO A PERSONAL IMPROVEMENT PL AN

If a personal improvement plan has been set for you, or you have set one for someone else, ensure that you make an effort to achieve what has been outlined in it. The manager should go over the goals of your plan, but only you can make the choice—and take the necessary action—to achieve them.

If you do not feel that your future lies with the company, inform your employer that you will not continue at the present organization, as this will save everyone time and energy. If you want to hold onto your job, look at the PIP as a positive thing. Remember, sometimes we need to learn from mistakes and useful feedback, and a PIP will help you do that.

HOW CAN I SURVIVE A PERFORMANCE IMPROVEMENT PL AN

Your PIP was created to help you make improvements. The end result is you become a more valuable, qualified employee. If you really want to survive your plan, or even make the most of it, try to:

Make your job a top priority, above all else!

Seek help when you need it, and don't sit on it if you are unsure as this will delay your progress Remain positive by ensuring your attitude doesn't change as a result. Simply pour your energy into making the improvements that you must make!

27

CORRECTING BEHAVIOUR THAT LASTS - TEMPLATE

*D*ealing with conflict is part of the job. Ensure that when you correct behavior, it has a lasting effect.

You will not have time to correct people repeatedly. You have other priorities. This chapter focuses on how to tweak behavior and make it stick long-term through conversations and accountability partners.

WHY IS BEHAVIORAL CHANGE DIFFICULT, AND WHY DO THESE CHANGES NEVER L AST IF DONE INCORRECTLY?

Underperformance is a tricky issue. Habits are often difficult to change but not impossible if done correctly. For example, a previous leader or manager may have allowed the team to work in a particular way that doesn't work for you.

When someone is used to behaving in a particular way, they may not see why they have to change. As a leader, you have to help them see! They may not take what you're saying seriously, and if you don't attempt to change the behavior in the long term, the 'old behaviors' will soon return. That's because long-term change takes time.

If you want to make a change, you must get your employee fully onboard. They need to be willing to invest their time and remain committed to making a change.

HOW CAN IT BE DONE EFFECTIVELY?

If your goal is to change behavior, give this template below a go. It's a good idea to first assess and communicate the issue to your employee before making a plan of action. Start by:

1. Identify the problematic behavior
2. Set a standard—how should they be behaving?
3. Set your goal, using the SMART framework
4. Have a conversation with your team member. Explain the problem, identify the correct behavior, talk about the goal you have set for them, and why it's important that they make the change.
5. Have regular progress reviews to check in on behavior and ensure that you provide training, instructions, or adequate resources to help support the employee in question.

Correction is part of the whole feedback process, more often than not, people want to do well and are therefore willing to work towards their improvement goal. If they are unwilling, a PIP will not help, and you will most likely need to get HR involved.

6. Always focus on the problem, not the actual person. The person is valuable, it's simply the error that needs correction. As a leader, it's your responsibility to make that distinction.

7. Don't hold grudges! Doing so will sour a positive atmosphere and create a negative, bitter environment. This could impact the progress of everyone on your team.

8. Do not lose your temper, be sarcastic, issue threats, reprimand, or humiliate your team members when correcting behavior. As a leader, you have a responsibility to maintain professionalism at all times. I know this is common sense, but you'd be surprised how many times it happens.

9. Assign an accountability buddy to keep the employee on track. This will help the employee not to feel as if they only have to answer to leaders and managers. Sometimes, this is a little more motivating and less formal. Making it easier for the employee to tackle the issue.

WHAT'S AN ACCOUNTABILITY PARTNER AND HOW CAN I BEST USE ONE?

An accountability partner is someone you team up with who is willing to hold you accountable for your actions and ensure you achieve your goals. In turn, you hold them accountable, as well. It's a partnership of sorts. Both parties help each other reach their end goals.

To utilize an accountability partner, an agreement is formed between the two parties. Honesty and integrity are crucial for this relationship to work, so it's important that both parties are open to giving and receiving truthful feedback. It's typical for the partners to meet up briefly on a weekly basis and discuss a goal or objective they want to achieve for that week, while also discussing their 'why'. You both check in at the end of the week to discuss your progress.

When checking in with an accountability partner, these are some questions you may want to consider:

- How do you feel your week went? What progress did you make?
- Is there anything you would've done differently? Did you achieve your goal?
- How did you/why didn't you achieve it? What was your biggest learning this week?

If you work with an accountability partner to tweak your behavior, ensure that you are consistent. Don't avoid them because you feel you haven't made the progress you expected to make! For this to work, everyone must be committed!

Accountability partners are a great incentive. If you are a busy leader (which you probably always are), it's useful to pair a couple of your team members together for peer support in this way. Changing behavior can take time, so be patient, ensure you remain supportive of your employees and check in with them on regular basis to assess their transformation.

You've now reached the end of section IV, which means you have lots of tools available to help you be an effective, innovative leader of today. Once you've read the conclusion, you're fully equipped to be the best female leader you can be... AND more!

You got this!

SCAN QR CODE FOR ALL PDFs

FINAL THOUGHTS

You've made it to the end of this book, which means you're armed with the strategies and tools you need to up your game as a defining female leader. As women, we have a huge responsibility. Why? Because our leadership style is so unique, we find ourselves working harder than ever to make it!

Throughout this book, you've explored your own leadership style while learning how to push your own boundaries. You've learned to lead yourself, your direct reports, and your team. By now, you should be putting what you've learned into practice—it's valuable, so why wait? Especially if you want to fast-track your career!

The key things you will have learned throughout this book are that:

- Age is just a number, and should never impact how successful you are as a leader
- Leadership starts by understanding your key attributes, you can use your strengths to lead individuals and your team, and excel in your leadership role
- Good feedback is important for growth— while yes, it should be positive, it should also be constructive and include some learning
- It's a good idea to get a mentor before you begin to coach or mentor others, as this will help you develop before you can truly develop others

In addition to this, recognize that you have everything it takes to be a dynamic and exceptional manager, and that talent should not be wasted!

While I know you're awesome already, I want to leave you with this final quote:

> *"If your actions create a legacy that inspires others to dream more, learn more, do more, and become more, then, you are an excellent leader"*
> ~ Dolly Parton

As you begin your journey as the next female leader, appreciate that you have already begun to inspire others and build your legacy. Therefore, it's your mission to do this continuously and consistently.

Do you remember how I told you at the beginning of this book that failure is not an option with me by your side?

Well, if you follow these 21 strategies, failure is NOT an option, because you are now ready to become a goal-driven, forward-thinking, action-oriented leader, and it's time to act right now...

1. Head over to the leadership style test. Figure out your leadership style and qualities so you can be the leader you're meant to be!
2. Use the templates in section IV to begin leading with purpose, confidence, and enthusiasm. Be ready to raise the next generation of leaders!

Now that you've read this book remember to leave your feedback on Amazon. *Simply scan the QR code below and leave your feedback now. It only takes 2 minutes, but it makes a world of difference to me and many other women who need this book right now so that they their leadership skills to the next level! Your feedback is so important and appreciated.*

As my parting gift to you, I'd like to leave you with this poem. May it inspire you to soar higher than you ever imagined possible.

(*This poem has been slightly modified to fit the female audience*)

The Woman Who Thinks She Can

*If you think you are beaten, you are If you
    think you dare not, you don't,*
*If you like to win, but you think you can't It is
    almost certain you won't.*
*If you think you'll lose, you're lost For out of
    the world we find, Success begins with a
    gal's will It's all in the state of mind.*
*If you think you are outclassed, you are You've
    got to think high to rise,*
*You've got to be sure of yourself before You can
    ever win a prize.*
*Life's battles don't always go To the stronger
    or faster woman,*
*But soon or late the woman who wins Is the
    woman who thinks she can.*
~ Walter D. Wintle

(Slightly modified for the female
    audience)

You are now ready to start your journey!

FROM THE AUTHOR

Thank you so much for reading 'Leadership For The New Female Manager'. Please remember to write a brief review at Amazon or wherever you purchased this book.

By now, I hope you are getting excited about all the possibilities that exist for you as a new manager. There is a lot to learn, but the journey is really rewarding. You will have the opportunity to help your team grow and develop into strong leaders, and in turn, you will conquer all your fears.

If this book helped you take the first steps toward becoming a better leader, *I invite you to take 2 minutes of your time and leave me your feedback. Please take 2 minutes of your time, and leave me your honest feedback.* You will help many other amazing, new female leaders decide to buy this book and learn how to make a difference truly. Your feedback can make that happen. So, don't wait; post your feedback now; even if you just give it 5 stars, that's enough for someone to choose this book and make a career-changing decision. You may not know that, for self-publishers, your feedback is really important. It helps us, authors spread the word about our books and it helps those who are looking to find our books when they need them most. I invite you to take **5 minutes right now, scan the QR code below with your phone camera and leave me your honest feedback.** I am really, really grateful.

JOIN OUR PRIVATE FACEBOOK GROUP

If you haven't already joined our amazing private Facebook Group of Women who are either starting their businesses or are already entrepreneurs, I invite you to join us. *Scan the QR code below with your phone camera.*

REMEMBER TO GRAB YOUR FREE GIFT

SPECIAL BONUS!

Want this cheatsheet for FREE?

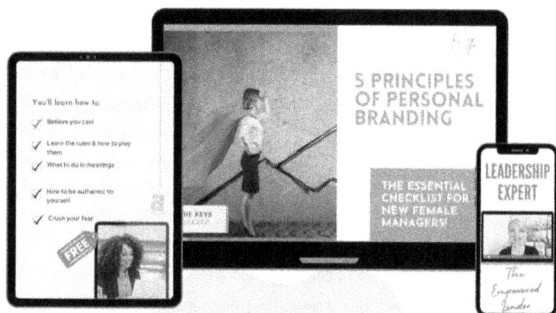

Get FREE unlimited access to it and all of
my books by joining our community!

**Scan with
your camera
to join!**

In the *5 Golden Rules to Personal Branding*, you'll find:

- The easy-to-follow golden rules will help you design your brand from scratch.
- My personal story took 20 years to develop through many mistakes, time, and sacrifice.
- Quick action steps that you can take right now to get started.

- A quick access to our community of amazing female leaders to help you form your tribe.

ABOUT THE AUTHOR

Karina is a certified Business Coach specializing in helping women entrepreneurs reach their full potential. She has helped hundreds of leaders and entrepreneurs reach for the stars and achieve personal and professional success. This is her true passion. She has helped countless female leaders overcome imposter syndrome, which kept them from achieving incredible results.

She has lived and worked internationally and has consulted in the retail, pharmaceutical, and financial industries, to name a few. Her energy and passion have brought a positive change within small and large teams alike. She has an uncanny ability to open minds to new and innovative ways of thinking, helping individuals reach their financial potential.

Over the last fifteen years, she has delivered many motivational keynotes in English, Spanish, Portuguese, and Polish.

She has written two bestselling books that have

generated 6-figure incomes for many female entrepreneurs working from the comfort of their own homes.

- facebook.com/Karina-G-Sanchez-Consulting-112840551328381
- instagram.com/karina.g.sanchez
- linkedin.com/in/karina-g-sanchez-0b446216
- youtube.com/@karinagsanchez
- tiktok.com/@karinag.sanchez

BIBLIOGRAPHY

Chapter 1

- https://www.investorsinpeople.com/knowledge/swot-analysis-understand-yourself-others/
- http://middlemanaged.com/2020/03/07/creating-a-swot-analysis-on-your-own-leadership-skills-and-abilities/

Chapter 2

- https://smallbusinessify.com/the-importance-of-self-confidence-in-leadership/
- https://www.pragmaticinstitute.com/resources/articles/product/12-ways-to-develop-leadership-confidence/
- https://www.benchmarkone.com/blog/9-leadership-exercises-to-help-your-confidence/

Chapter 3

- https://medium.com/@betsyallenmanning/3-proven-strategies-to-gain-credibility-respect-and-influence-as-a-new-leader-4dd7c8713172
- https://blog.hubspot.com/marketing/build-credibility-new-leader
- https://www.indeed.com/career-advice/career-development/types-of-power-in-leadership

Chapter 4

- https://www.prileadership.com/news/2019/3/17/speak-up-how-to-gain-visibility-for-yourself-amp-support-visibility-for-others
- https://www.prileadership.com/news/2019/4/2/speak-up-practice
- https://www.prileadership.com/news/2019/4/3/speak-up-present-article-3-in-series

Chapter 5

- https://www.blackenterprise.com/5-ways-young-leaders-can-gain-respect-and-influence/

Chapter 6

- https://www.insperity.com/blog/how-to-be-a-confident-boss-without-sounding-like-a-jerk/

Chapter 7

- https://mindfulambition.net/power-of-perception/
- https://www.usmcu.edu/Portals/218/Leaders%20How%20Do%20You%20Manage%20Perception.pdf
- https://www.vantageleadership.com/our-blog/others-perception-reality-change/

Chapter 8

- http://www.nwlink.com/~donclark/leader/leadhb.html

Chapter 9

- https://www.elevatecorporatetraining.com.au/2019/04/
  09/7-strategies-good-leaders-can-use-to-give-feedback/

Chapter 10

- https://www.skillcast.com/blog/8-steps-authentic-
  leadership
- https://www.forbes.com/sites/forbescoachescouncil/
  2018/03/13/seven-ways-to-develop-your-authentic-
  leadership-style/?sh=24c396c069e6

Chapter 11

- https://marketinginsidergroup.com/marketing-strategy/
  help-your-employees-feel-safe-and-unleash-the-power-
  of-employee-activation/

Chapter 12

- https://blog.smarp.com/10-ways-to-foster-upward-
  communication-in-the-workplace
- https://www.ckju.net/en/dossier/challenges-and-
  enablers-upward-communication-how-foster-speak-
  culture-your-organization/1256
- https://blog.smarp.com/10-ways-to-foster-upward-
  communication-in-the-workplace

Chapter 13

- https://www.eaglesflight.com/blog/the-importance-of-delegation-for-leadership

- https://hbr.org/2017/10/to-be-a-great-leader-you-have-to-learn-how-to-delegate-well

Chapter 14

- https://www.quantumworkplace.com/employee-recognition
- https://neilpatel.com/blog/employee-spotlights/
- https://www.quantumworkplace.com/employee-recognition

Chapter 15
- https://www.ellevatenetwork.com/articles/7542-11-steps-to-creating-a-shared-vision-for-your-team

Chapter 16

- https://getlighthouse.com/blog/managing-a-new-team/
- https://www.forbes.com/sites/forbeshumanresourcescouncil/2018/03/05/10-simple-ways-to-get-to-know-your-employees-better/?sh=730a3df44b97

Chapter 17

- https://www.forbes.com/sites/forbescoachescouncil/2016/09/14/13-ways-leaders-can-better-understand-the-unique-strengths-of-their-team-members/?sh=6f0cb3232a51
- https://high5test.com/team-strengths/

Chapter 18

- https://www.thoughtfulleader.com/roles-and-responsibilities/
- https://www.indeed.com/career-advice/career-development/team-roles-and-responsibilities

Chapter 19

- https://www.quantumworkplace.com/future-of-work/how-to-align-organizational-goals
- https://www.bizjournals.com/houston/blog/2014/12/5-methods-to-align-company-and-personal-goals.html

Chapter 20

- The Leader as Coach (hbr.org)

Chapter 21

- https://www.ccl.org/articles/leading-effectively-articles/build-trust-in-the-workplace/
- https://www.achievers.com/blog/building-trust-workplace/

Chapter 22

- https://www.indeed.com/career-advice/career-development/10-common-leadership-styles

Chapter 23

- https://www.thebalancecareers.com/coaching-questions-for-managers-2275913

Chapter 24

- https://www.businessnewsdaily.com/9451-clear-employee-expectations.html

Chapter 25

- https://www.indeed.com/hire/c/info/individual-development-plan-examples

Chapter 26

- https://www.valamis.com/hub/performance-improvement-plan

Image Credits
Chapter 20

- https://hbr.org/2019/11/the-leader-as-coach